The Text of
A MODEL ZONING ORDINANCE

With Commentary, by

Fred H. Bair, Jr.
Planning Consultant,
Auburndale, Florida

and

Ernest R. Bartley
Professor of Political Science,
University of Florida, and
Planning Consultant

THIRD EDITION, 1966

AMERICAN SOCIETY OF PLANNING OFFICIALS

1313 EAST SIXTIETH STREET • CHICAGO, ILLINOIS 60637

Third Edition

Copyright 1960, 1966 American Society of Planning Officials

Library of Congress Catalog Card No. 60-14648

$5.00

K

B163
T3
C.2

CONTENTS

iii

FOREWORD

The first edition of the *Text of A Model Zoning Ordinance With Commentary*, published in 1958 by the University of Florida Public Administration Clearing Service, sold out in a few months. The second edition, slightly revised, was published by the American Society of Planning Officials in 1960 and those 2,500 copies were sold out by 1964.

This third edition has been extensively revised on the basis of five more years of experience on the part of the authors, plus comments, criticism, and suggestions by planners, lawyers, and laymen interested in zoning. Still, it is fundamentally the same book that appeared in 1958; the basic *Text* has worn well during the eight years since it was first published. And the comment I made in the Foreword to the 1960 edition remains pertinent.

At the office of the American Society of Planning Officials we have been suspicious of any "models" for planning, and particularly of any "model zoning ordinance." When the review copy of the Bair-Bartley pamphlet appeared we were forced to change our minds. In the first place, this *Text* offered no samples or models of district regulations— and these are by far the most dangerous part of an ordinance to copy. In the second place, the text was based on the *Standard State Zoning Enabling Act*, which has been used in nearly every state as the basis for zoning enabling legislation. And in the third place, anyone who read the commentary carefully, and was guided by it, would not copy slavishly.

During these eight years, the *Text of A Model Zoning Ordinance* has had great influence in improving the quality of zoning ordinances in the United States. The third edition will undoubtedly extend that influence. However, the third edition will eventually go out of print as its predecessors did, and this is as it should be. A truism in zoning administration is that the zoning ordinance should be completely reviewed for revision every five years. This statement applies equally to a hypothetical zoning ordinance, the model text in this book.

DENNIS O'HARROW
Executive Director
American Society of Planning Officials

ix

PREFACE

When we first began to work with the idea of standardizing the text of a zoning ordinance, we had no idea of the chains we were fashioning for ourselves. As the work progressed to publication in 1958 of the first edition by the University of Florida Public Administration Clearing Service, we nurtured a small hope that the work might have some local impact.

We candidly admit that we were surprised and pleased at the reception accorded our efforts. Our file of letters regarding the first edition of the *Text* attained sizable proportions.

The second edition of the *Text* was published in 1960 by the American Society of Planning Officials. Again the reaction, at least that to which we admit, was favorable. A third edition is now required and the chains of publication bind us tightly.

Any improvements that may be noted in this third edition over earlier efforts are the direct result of the comments, suggestions, and criticisms made of the first and second editions. Some improvements may be the result, too, of the fact that each of us may have learned something about zoning in the past seven years of practice.

We trust that this third edition will inspire further analysis and critique to the end that further improvements in the field of zoning technique will result.

It is with a sense of deep appreciation that we acknowledge our debt to all of those who have aided us in the learning process—professional planners, city councilmen and county commissioners, judges and lawyers, planning board and board of adjustment members, zoning administrators, and interested laymen. We particularly wish to thank the following persons:

Mr. Fred G. Stickel, III, Counselor at Law, and Chairman, Committee on Zoning and Planning, National Institute of Municipal Law Officers;

Mr. Ronald Scott, Director of Planning, Greensboro, North Carolina;

Mr. Philip P. Green, Jr., Assistant Director, Institute of Government, University of North Carolina;

Mr. Dennis O'Harrow, Executive Director, American Society of Planning Officials;

Mr. Jack Noble, Assistant Director, American Society of Planning Officials;

Mr. Osee R. Fagan, City Attorney, Gainesville, Florida.

We are honored by the publication of this third edition by the American Society of Planning Officials.

For the errors of interpretation or fact that remain, we absolve our gracious critics and ASPO.

FRED H. BAIR, JR.
ERNEST R. BARTLEY

INTRODUCTION

Modern American man is highly dependent on his fellows. This is the source of both his strength and his weakness. He no longer produces the basic necessities of his daily existence—his food, his clothes, his house—but these necessities are supplied to him more abundantly than ever before.

Growing interdependence, technological advances, and changes in methods of production and distribution have accelerated migration to cities, and the involved structure of modern society becomes increasingly complex. With complexity mounting, with isolated independence giving way to urban interdependence, an inevitable result is the need for regulation by government of a sizable number of activities. It becomes necessary to limit some rights of property in order that the general welfare may be protected.

Zoning, a tool of modern planning, is one of innumerable dramatic manifestations of growth of government controls in response to urban needs. The *power* to zone arises from the police power—the power of government to protect the citizens. The *need* to zone arises because humanity clustered in cities demands a form of protection which is of no importance to humanity dispersed.

In the present phase of zoning—and it is still in its infancy—regulation takes the form of dividing the city into districts, and within each district limiting the height, bulk, and use of buildings and other structures, the density of population, the use to which land may be put, and other matters. Such regulation must not be arbitrary or capricious. It must have a substantial relation to the general public welfare. It must be in accordance with a comprehensive plan.[1] Zoning is thus the subordination of personal interests to what is determined, through procedures established by law, to be the public interest.

---

[1] The term "comprehensive plan" very probably meant in the early days of zoning only that there should not be piecemeal zoning—that the ordinance should be geographically comprehensive in the sense that *all* of the area of the political jurisdiction should be zoned. More recently some courts have been persuaded that a "comprehensive plan" is the studied document prepared by planners setting forth a balanced pattern of objectives and policies for future development. See, *e.g., Eves v. Zoning Board of Adjustment*, 401 Pa. 211, 164 A.2d 7 (1960).

Zoning ordinances which are not *geographically* comprehensive have generally fallen in court attacks. Those which are not in accord with a planner's comprehensive plan have in increasing numbers been invalidated by the courts. See RHYNE, MUNICIPAL LAW (1957), 818, and cases therein cited.

1

Zoning is increasingly under attack as a form of unnecessarily rigid regulation rooted in outmoded tradition and inhibiting desirable change and experimentation. Many of these criticisms are made by planners. The fault, however, does not lie with zoning, which can be a very flexible instrument, but with failure to take advantage of its flexibility. Attacks are generally against zoning of 30 years ago which still remains in effect, rather than against zoning as it could, and should, be. Planning and zoning commissions, professional planning staff members, consultants, and administrative officials cling to past forms because they are familiar, tested, and comfortable. Makeshift change is piled on makeshift change to make the least adjustment possible to keep the antiquated machinery running somehow; there are not nearly enough complete overhauls.

Growth of cities is not confined to metropolitan areas; increases have taken place in most small- and medium-sized cities all over the nation. The need for sound and well administered zoning ordinances in these communities is most pressing, yet governmental officials and citizens are not always certain as to how to proceed. The financial and technical resources in the planning field, so readily available in the large metropolitan areas, are not usually present in smaller cities. Many such cities have not been at all certain as to how to utilize the power to zone which is granted to them by general state act and, in some states, by special legislation as well.[2]

When cities have zoned, therefore, they have far too often adopted a zoning ordinance lamentably deficient in many respects. Some ordinances have been copied from sources whose chief recommendation has been that they were available from a nearby town. Many ordinances now in effect are invalid in large or small part because the basic enabling act was ignored or its provisions altered out of recognizable shape. A large number of ordinances show poor original organization

---

[2] It is a long accepted rule that a municipality possesses only those powers that the state has specifically granted to it or those that may be reasonably implied therefrom. Such grants of authority may be accomplished by general or special act.

The power to zone is conferred on municipalities by one form or another of general statute in all states. Additionally, in a number of states, the legislature may expand, limit, or qualify such zoning authority by special act applicable to a specific city. The special act mechanism, once the accepted method for creating state-municipal relationships, is fortunately becoming less common.

See SWARTHOUT AND BARTLEY, PRINCIPLES AND PROBLEMS OF STATE AND LOCAL GOVERNMENT (1958), 177-9, 187-9.

and draftsmanship, drip unnecessary and confusing language, and are patched, amended, and padded to the point where even those who administer them do not know what some sections mean (or in some cases whether certain sections are or are not in effect).

There is vast and general confusion about the roles of the city council, the building inspector, the zoning commission, and the planning board (if any). And the board of adjustment, which under even the best circumstances can become what Walter Blucher, noted planning authority, has called the "slow leak in zoning," has sometimes reached the point where it is a full-scale blowout. So serious has the situation of boards of adjustment become that Grady Clay, public spirited journalist with an acute awareness of planning's strengths and weaknesses, has referred to the boards as "zoning chiropractors manipulating the backbone of zoning until it has no spine left."

There is plenty of reason to believe that most of the errors in drafting, substance, and administration of zoning ordinances are not errors of intent or venality. Rather they arise, usually, from a failure to try to get correct information or from misinformation, lack of information, or an absolutely baffling tendency to copy the worst practices in nearby cities. The errors remain because of an obstinate reluctance to rock the boat by making the needed changes or performing the necessary drastic overhaul.

Viewed substantively, it is a rare ordinance indeed that does not commit greatly excessive land areas to commercial or industrial use, thereby ensuring that the land so classified will not be used for much of anything or that in the spotty development that does result large sections of the community will be permanently blighted. It is a rare ordinance that does not strip zone for commercial use the land along major thoroughfares, even though every objective study since World War II has demonstrated clearly that strip type commercial developments are now generally functionally obsolete and are likely to result in business failures, community blight, increased traffic hazards, and other problems. It is a rare zoning ordinance that does not try to use the zoning power to regulate problems that should be regulated under other city powers; most cities expect, and try to make, zoning do "too much."

This publication is essentially an effort to draft *only the text* of a model zoning ordinance which can be adopted by small- and medium-sized cities in those states where general (or special) enabling legislation is based on the *Standard State Zoning Enabling Act*.[3] Since the influence of the *Standard Act* was so great, adopted as it was by so many states, this text of a model zoning ordinance hopefully should have a wide applicability.

The Contents of a Modern Zoning Ordinance

It should be emphasized that what is discussed here is primarily the text of the zoning ordinance. A complete ordinance includes two other vital elements: (1) the schedule of district regulations[4] and (2) the official zoning map.

The zoning map, which shows the boundaries of districts, and the schedule of district regulations, which sets forth the requirements and prohibitions for the individual districts, *must* be developed in the individual communities to meet local needs. These things cannot be standardized.

The text of the ordinance is something else again; it deals largely with procedural, administrative, and legal matters, and with definitions of terms usually used in zoning. Since the basic enabling legislation which gives rise to most municipal zoning is the same, and since courts have tested and interpreted the language of the basic act, there seems to be no reason why the text of a local zoning ordinance cannot be standardized. This we have attempted to do.

The model text provided here may still need minor adjustment to local circumstances—for example, there is no point in referring to railroad lines in relation to district boundaries if there is no railroad in the community. But, on the whole, this text should enable the city to move forward more rapidly to the matters which require intensive local study—the schedule of district regulations and the official zoning map.

It is essential to emphasize that zoning and planning are not the

---

[3] Advisory Committee on Zoning, United States Department of Commerce, A STANDARD STATE ZONING ENABLING ACT UNDER WHICH MUNICIPALITIES MAY ADOPT ZONING REGULATIONS (revised edition, 1926). The text of this epochal work is reprinted in Appendix A of this publication. See pp. 89–93.
This work will be cited hereafter as the *Standard Act*.

[4] A schedule of district regulations presents, in tabular and easy to understand form, the regulations applicable to each particular zoning classification. For a brief discussion on how to set up a schedule of district regulations for a small- or medium-sized city, see Appendix B, pp. 93–98.

same thing. Zoning is but one of the planning controls, or planning tools. It is an extremely important one[5] but it is not planning, nor does it cover anything like the total scope of controls needed to guide and ensure sound development. We urge the importance of more comprehensive planning; it is, indeed, at least legally questionable for a municipality acting under the powers granted by the *Standard Act* to adopt a zoning ordinance without first having drafted a comprehensive plan.[6]

The Legal Foundation of the Model Text

The model text, as drafted in the pages that follow, is based on the *Standard Act*. The fact that so many states have adopted it, in whole or in substantial part, and the fact that even special acts have most frequently been based on it, means that little conflict should arise in those states utilizing both a general enabling act and the device of special legislation.

In case of possible conflict between state zoning enabling legislation and a city charter or special act on the point, we are of the opinion that the safer course to take in such circumstances usually is to follow the language and requirements of the general act. The high courts of the various states have interpreted most of its provisions, thus giving the municipality using it some measure of assurance as to possible future interpretations that may be placed on its language. Because of the widespread use of the *Standard Act*, legislative language is similar from state to state. Judicial pronouncements in one state are, under such circumstances, often applied by the courts in another.[7]

[5] BARTLEY AND BOYER, MUNICIPAL ZONING: FLORIDA LAW AND PRACTICE (1950), 9–10; BARTLEY, *Legal Problems in Florida Municipal Zoning,* 6 FLA. L. R. (1953), 356.

[6] *Standard Act,* sec. 3. The requirement, it is true, has unfortunately been honored more in the breach than the observance, but zoning ordinances have been held invalid in a number of states because they were not enacted in accordance with a comprehensive plan. See footnote 1, supra, and RHYNE, MUNICIPAL LAW (1957), 818, and cases therein cited.

The fact that a zoning ordinance should be, legally and logically, based on a comprehensive plan does *not* mean that the comprehensive plan is thereafter immutable and unchangeable. Planning is, or most definitely ought to be, a continuous process. Detailed long-range planning is well-nigh impossible because of advances in technology, if for no other reason.

[7] Such authority is known to lawyers as "extra-jurisdictional" authority. Technically, of course, the courts in one state are not bound by the decisions of the courts of another. Where the language of the basic statute is the same or similar, however, such decisions can properly be called to a court's attention and may be persuasive.

Certainly any city contemplating the use of the model text should check carefully any charter provision or special local legislative authorization to zone. If the conflict between the general enabling act and the special authorization is procedural, nothing will normally be lost by following the more restrictive requirements. Thus the *Standard Act*, section 4, requires 15 days notice of public hearing. If the city charter requires 20 days, the safe course of action is to adhere to the 20-day requirement.[8]

The model text contains a number of new ideas and innovations, each carefully considered for legality within the framework of the *Standard Act*. These new concepts will be noted in the commentary and discussion that follow each section of the model ordinance. It is well to remember that law is a dynamic and constantly evolving thing; the fact that an idea is relatively untried does not automatically mean that it is illegal. Zoning law and administration must accommodate to the demands and changes of urban need.

Sources for Materials Included in the Model Text

Aside from the legal sources of the *Standard Act*, the general enabling acts of the states, and judicial pronouncements, the form, language, and content of the model text stem from many origins. In the monthly publication *Florida Planning and Development*, new approaches to meet new needs have been developed and reported.[9] Much of the material has previously appeared in this publication. Any current zoning ordinance which is carefully drafted owes a heavy debt of gratitude to the Planning Advisory Service publications of the American Society of Planning Officials. And we have added elements based on our own extensive practical experience in the field.

Thus this text represents a combination of material which in our opinion is the best available from other sources or the best which could be devised when other sources left something to be desired. It is not the last word. Suggestions for further revision and improvement will be greatly appreciated.

---

[8] In those states using both general and special legislation, there is no very concrete indication as to whether the general or the special zoning legislation takes precedence. In most possible instances of conflict, the order of precedence is, at best, confusing.

[9] This publication was formerly issued by the Florida Planning and Zoning Association. It is now edited and published independently by Fred H. Bair, Jr., Post Office Box 828, Auburndale, Florida.

Form of Presentation of the Model Text

Each section of the model text is followed by commentary and discussion; sometimes that commentary and discussion is quite lengthy. The purpose of these explanatory notes is twofold. In the first place, we have tried to explain why we have done certain things in order to inform interested persons about the meaning and purposes of individual sections. In the second place, we recognize that some portions of the text, if enacted, may be litigated. If so, the explanations given can well serve as a basis for a showing of intent and purpose.

We would emphasize again that the text is a model for small- and medium-sized cities; broader generalization is possible for these cities than would be true in the case of great metropolitan communities where more detail and specification would be necessary. No person should be led, however, into presuming that the model text, as here given, should be enacted verbatim. Changes may be necessary from community to community. Some will be changes in terminology: some cities call their governing body a "council," some a "commission," and some a "board of managers." Some cities will need to make changes in substance to adjust provisions to local circumstances or to particular requirements of enabling legislation at variance with the *Standard Act*.

We recognized, in setting out the form and phraseology of the model text, that small- and medium-sized cities do not, as a general rule, have available full-time municipal legal and planning staffs. Municipal attorneys serving many such towns are not specialists in public law; their governmental duties are auxiliary to their private law practice. The officer enforcing the zoning ordinance may have this function as one of several duties he performs for the city government. The language of the text, therefore, has been geared insofar as possible to easy understanding with a minimum of study on the part of the persons who will be charged with its administration and enforcement. One may note, too, that understandable language plays its part in making it easier for the citizen to understand his rights under the ordinance. The wording of the text, taken in conjunction with the explanatory material should give a clear picture of the intent and purpose of our efforts.

Zoning and Litigation

The possibility always exists that a zoning ordinance, or more probably some section of it, will at some future date be the subject of litigation. Thus the drafting of a zoning ordinance needs to take into consideration such a possibility. This model text has been scrutinized to the best of our abilities to ensure that it meets constitutional and legal requirements. Yet those who have any familiarity with the processes and functioning of the law will recognize that it is impossible to foresee all the possible legal interpretations that courts may place on an ordinance.

A well-drafted ordinance, of course, is less likely to be litigated than one poorly drawn. Clear and precise language will avoid legal pitfalls in most instances. The purpose of good zoning law and administration is to avoid litigation, not to encourage it.

It is well to remember, too, that most disputes, whether public or private, are usually settled out of court. Only a small percentage of arguments that *might* possibly get into court ever actually arrive before a judge for decision. One should not, therefore, draft a zoning ordinance *solely* with the aim of possible litigation in view. The emphasis our society places upon law sometimes leads to this result. The best rule to follow in this regard is to look to the *possibility* and not the *probability* of litigation.

The model text places very considerable emphasis upon following proper procedures in zoning administration. Procedure is important, for careful examination of the cases where zoning ordinances, or sections of them, have been declared invalid or unconstitutional will show that the majority of such declarations were based on matters of procedure. Proper procedures, including the careful and complete maintenance of required records pertaining to the administration of a zoning ordinance, will greatly diminish the possible areas of litigation.

Ordinances perfectly drafted and administered may still, however, be declared invalid if called in question before the courts. Hundreds of instances around the nation can be cited where zoning regulations have been found invalid because such regulations were "arbitrary, capricious, and unreasonable." Without becoming involved in a lengthy legal explanation, let it be forcefully noted that a zoning regulation must meet the test of *reasonableness*. There must be a reason for each zoning regulation, and that reason must bear a sound and defensible relationship to the public health, safety, morals, welfare, or good order. Zoning regulations must be based on and directly related to demonstrable and valid public interest.[10]

Sadly, but not surprisingly, zoning regulations sometimes use the phrases "public interest," "public purpose," or "public welfare" to cover personal prejudice, greed, or interest. Zoning *has* been used to make housing as expensive as possible in order to maximize tax return, to cut down the number of children in order to keep school costs low, to keep out small houses, and so forth. When used for such purposes, zoning can scarcely be said to be "reasonable."

Far too many cities are afraid of litigation and abjectly give in to any applicant who screams that he "will take the city to court." (Sometimes, of course, these fears are justified!) But the expense to a city in winning a noteworthy case will in almost every instance be more than repaid in future zoning troubles avoided. A properly drafted zoning ordinance, correctly administered, and based on demonstrable public interest is impossible to attack in court if the city has properly prepared its defense.[11]

[10] For lawyers who may read this material, we note that they are well aware that in most jurisdictions zoning regulations are presumptively valid and the plaintiff attacking the ordinance carries the burden of proof in showing that the regulation is "arbitrary, capricious, and unreasonable." Most jurisdictions also will hold a zoning regulation valid if it is said to be "fairly debatable." Properly utilized, these principles give the city a great edge in any court action brought against it.

[11] Each of the authors has appeared in court many times as expert witness both on the side of local governments and for private parties attacking zoning regulations.

THE TEXT OF A MODEL ZONING ORDINANCE WITH COMMENTARY

In the materials that follow, the text of the model zoning ordinance is set in large type. Each section of the model text is followed by commentary and discussion in smaller type.

THE TEXT OF A MODEL ZONING ORDINANCE
WITH COMMENTARY

ORDINANCE NO. _____

AN ORDINANCE ESTABLISHING COMPREHENSIVE ZONING REGULATIONS FOR THE CITY OF _____, AND PROVIDING FOR THE ADMINISTRATION, ENFORCEMENT, AND AMENDMENT THEREOF, IN ACCORDANCE WITH THE PROVISIONS OF CHAPTER _____, STATE STATUTES, AND FOR THE REPEAL OF ALL ORDINANCES IN CONFLICT HEREWITH

Whereas Chapter _____, State Statutes, empowers the City to enact a zoning ordinance and to provide for its administration, enforcement, and amendment, and

Whereas the City Council deems it necessary, for the purpose of promoting the health, safety, morals, or general welfare of the city to enact such an ordinance, and

Whereas the City Council, pursuant to the provisions of Chapter _____, State Statutes, has appointed a Zoning Commission to recommend the boundaries of the various original districts and appropriate regulations to be enforced therein, and

Whereas the Zoning Commission has divided the city into districts and has prepared regulations pertaining to such districts in accordance with a comprehensive plan and designed to lessen congestion in the streets; to secure safety from fire, panic, and other dangers; to promote health and the general welfare; to provide adequate light and air; to prevent the overcrowding of land; to avoid undue concentration of population; to facilitate the adequate provision of transportation, water, sewerage, schools, parks, and other public requirements, and

Whereas the Zoning Commission has given reasonable consideration, among other things, to the character of the districts and their peculiar suitability for particular uses, with a view to conserving the value of buildings and encouraging the most appropriate use of land throughout the municipality, and

Whereas the Zoning Commission has made a preliminary report and held public hearings thereon, and submitted its final report to the City Council, and

13

Whereas the City Council has given due public notice of hearings relating to zoning districts, regulations, and restrictions, and has held such public hearings, and

Whereas all requirements of Chapter _____, State Statutes, with regard to the preparation of the report of the Zoning Commission and subsequent action of the City Council have been met;

NOW THEREFORE BE IT ORDAINED BY THE PEOPLE OF THE CITY OF _____, State:

COMMENTARY—PREAMBLE

Those persons familiar with modern legislative drafting techniques will recognize that the model ordinance contains an unusually long preamble or preface. The modern tendency is toward very short preambles or toward eliminating them altogether, retaining the enacting clause as the only language that precedes the first section or article of a bill or ordinance. A preamble is not an essential part of an ordinance; it is in law, at best, but a guidepost to judicial interpretation. Yet a preamble can serve useful, though in many respects non-legal, purposes.

The older practice of a lengthy preamble has been incorporated in the model text for several reasons. It serves its traditional function of describing the purpose of the ordinance and making general reference to its objects. The preamble discloses the intention of the city council in enacting the ordinance. As an indication of the intent of the framers of the ordinance, the preamble can be a guide to the people generally and to the courts, a key to open the door to understanding.

The preamble of the text of the model ordinance has been drafted to accord with the *Standard Act.* The preamble is a recital that the city has, in fact, done the things necessary to comply with the procedural and substantive requirements prerequisite to the adoption of the zoning ordinance. Such a recital provides the city fathers with a check list of procedures and requirements that must be followed, just as the pilot of a modern airplane follows a check list to be certain he will not overlook some important phase of his procedure. Throughout the preamble, it is made clear that it is the intent of the city to utilize its authority in full conformity with state enabling legislation. The preamble thus serves as an educational and informational medium to the general citizenry, interested parties, the city's governing body, and the courts.

The language of the preamble follows closely the precise wording of the appropriate sections of the *Standard Act.* The first clause indicates the city's intent to avail itself of the grant of power to zone comprehensively, specifically the grant of section 1 of the *Standard Act.* The second clause sets out that the city deems the utilization of such authority a necessary exercise of its police power, as authorized in section 1. The third clause states the compliance of the city with the requirement of section 6 of the *Standard Act* that a zoning commission be established. The fourth and fifth clauses are taken almost verbatim from section 3 of the *Standard Act* and state the purposes of making the regulations.

The sixth clause of the model text recites that the zoning commission has made its recommendations and held its public hearings as required by section 6 of the *Standard Act*. The seventh clause demonstrates that the governing board of the municipality has fulfilled its share of the preliminary obligations under section 6. The last clause declares that, all of the prerequisites of state enabling legislation having been met, the city is now ready to enact a comprehensive zoning ordinance.

If the *Standard Act* is not used, the language of the preamble should be modified to track the specific language of the enabling act.

SECTION 1. ESTABLISHMENT OF DISTRICTS: PROVISION FOR OFFICIAL ZONING MAP

1. *Official Zoning Map.*—The city is hereby divided into zones, or districts, as shown on the Official Zoning Map which, together with all explanatory matter thereon, is hereby adopted by reference and declared to be a part of this ordinance.

The Official Zoning Map shall be identified by the signature of the Mayor attested by the City Clerk, and bearing the seal of the city under the following words: "This is to certify that this is the Official Zoning Map referred to in Section 1 of Ordinance Number _____ of the City of _____, State," together with the date of the adoption of this ordinance.

If, in accordance with the provisions of this ordinance and Chapter _____, State Statutes, changes are made in district boundaries or other matter portrayed on the Official Zoning Map, such changes shall be entered on the Official Zoning Map promptly after the amendment has been approved by the City Council, with an entry on the Official Zoning Map as follows: "On [*date*], by official action of the City Council, the following [change] changes were made in the Official Zoning Map: [*brief description of nature of change*]," which entry shall be signed by the Mayor and attested by the City Clerk. No amendment to this ordinance which involves matter portrayed on the Official Zoning Map shall become effective until after such change and entry has been made on said map.

No changes of any nature shall be made in the Official Zoning Map or matter shown thereon except in conformity with the procedures set forth in this ordinance. Any unauthorized change of whatever kind by any person or persons shall be considered a violation of this ordinance and punishable as provided under Section 16.

Regardless of the existence of purported copies of the Official Zoning Map which may from time to time be made or published, the Official Zoning Map which shall be located in the office of the City Clerk [or specify other place easily accessible to the public] shall be the final authority as to the current zoning status of land and water areas, buildings, and other structures in the city.

2. *Replacement of Official Zoning Map.*—In the event that the Official Zoning Map becomes damaged, destroyed, lost, or difficult to interpret because of the nature or number of changes and additions, the City Council may by resolution adopt a new Official Zoning Map which shall supersede the prior Official Zoning Map. The new Official Zoning Map may correct drafting or other errors or omissions in the prior Official Zoning Map, but no such correction shall have the effect of amending the original Official Zoning Map or any subsequent amendment thereof. The new Official Zoning Map shall be identified by the signature of the Mayor attested by the City Clerk, and bearing the seal of the city under the following words: "This is to certify that this Official Zoning Map supersedes and replaces the Official Zoning Map adopted [*date of adoption of map being replaced*] as part of Ordinance No. _____ of the City of _____, State."

Unless the prior Official Zoning Map has been lost, or has been totally destroyed, the prior map or any significant parts thereof remaining, shall be preserved, together with all available records pertaining to its adoption or amendment.

COMMENTARY—SECTION 1

The official zoning map is an integral part of modern zoning law and administration. The first paragraph of this section provides for dividing the city into districts and drawing the boundary lines of the districts on the official zoning map. There is nothing particularly new in the use of a zoning map; indeed, it has become standard practice. We would note, however, that as recently as 1958 we were shown an ordinance drawn in 1957 which attempted to outline the districts *verbally*, according to various street and ownership lines!

The official zoning map and its explanatory material is declared to be a part of the over-all zoning ordinance. Such adoption by reference and the use of a map as a part of the over-all ordinance have been held valid by the courts.

The worth of the official zoning map will depend upon a number of factors.

The city base map must, first of all, be accurately prepared; far too many cities have attempted to undertake zoning with an inaccurate map. No city should be without an accurate and current base map. Such a map is required for engineering and general administrative purposes. If no base map is available, zoning may serve in some instances as a stimulus for securing it—with consequent benefit to all phases of city government. There are various ways in which a good base map can be obtained; it makes very little sense to attempt to zone comprehensively without a good base map or, in the less satisfactory alternative, an aerial photo in place of a map.

To be meaningful the official zoning map must be of reasonably large scale. The original district boundaries must be drawn accurately. *The official zoning map must be kept current and no unauthorized changes must be allowed.* It must be easily accessible to the public. This section of the model text makes these aims mandatory.

The various signatures and certifications required in the second paragraph of subsection 1, once considered fairly novel or ignored, are now quite standard. The material of the third paragraph of subsection 1 is, however, relatively new. This portion deals with changes that must be made in the official zoning map when amendments to the basic ordinance are passed which change the boundaries of the various districts. If the official zoning map is supposed to set out the district boundaries, it follows that any changes should not be effective until they have been placed on the map. Otherwise a hiatus could easily occur; the city council might adopt an amendment but between the adoption and the time the change was placed on the map some person might buy property relying on the official zoning map, or the zoning enforcement officer might issue a permit relying on the map. This paragraph of the model ordinance seeks to make certain (1) that the change is made promptly on the map; (2) that the change is duly certified and noted as such; and (3) that the change shall not become effective until placed on the official zoning map.

The rights of persons are thus protected. The public will not be presumed to know that an amendment in district lines has been passed until the change has been properly recorded on the official zoning map. The requirements ensure that citizens can rely on the zoning map as a correct and up-to-date portrayal of the status of district boundaries. The requirements guarantee that a citizen has rights on which he can rely as of the time he looks at the official zoning map. We gave consideration to adding a requirement that the city council, in the amending ordinance, specify a date upon which the change was to be recorded on the map. This requirement was dropped, however, because of possible administrative difficulties in small towns; the official charged with changing the map, for example, might fall ill. Actually, in small- and medium-sized cities the city governing board customarily meets in the city hall in close proximity to the place where the official zoning map will be kept; under such circumstances the usual and preferred procedure would be to change the zoning map immediately following the adoption of the amendment.

The fourth paragraph of subsection 1 contains the usual penalty provisions for unauthorized alterations of the zoning map. It specifies that the penalties are those of Section 16 of the text of the model ordinance.

The last paragraph of subsection 1 establishes one official location and place for the *one* official zoning map. It should be obvious that there can be but one official map; the alternative is confusion at best and chaos at worst. It is obvious also that the citizens should know where the map is located and should have access to it at any time during business hours. Strangely enough, most of these very practical and common-sense features are not always found in modern zoning ordinances.

Subsection 2 sets up guidelines for replacing the official zoning map. The importance of maintaining a clear record as to changes in the map has already been stressed; over a period of years the official map may, because of numbers of changes, become difficult to interpret. Fire or natural catastrophe may even destroy it. It is well to set out by ordinance the procedure for adopting a new official zoning map, in case the original is destroyed or becomes unusable.

The superseded map or any portion of it should, under no circumstances, be destroyed. Possible future litigation may demand its use. It should be carefully preserved, together with the records of the city council regarding it.

In cities with large land areas (and surprisingly enough there are cities small in population with large, mostly uninhabited, land areas), or in counties using the model text as a basis for action, an official zoning atlas rather than a single official zoning map may be necessary. If an atlas is used, each sheet should be properly authenticated in the manner shown.

A final word is necessary concerning this section. We are well aware of the legal principle that one legislative body may not bind a future legislative body. Such a statement is technically correct and questions might, therefore, be raised concerning the legality and propriety of including restrictions of the type noted.

In actual practice, there are many phases of governmental activity where one legislative body effectively, though not legally, binds a future body to a particular course of action. It is obvious that a city council, having adopted this section of the model text may later amend and throw it out. Viewed in this light, the language might be, perhaps, more properly a part of general state enabling legislation. Yet we would insist that the language has a political utility. And once adopted, legal rights to use of property would vest rights that could not be disturbed except by subsequent valid amendatory action by the City Council. We would argue in strongest terms for the approach taken here. In our view the practical advantages to be derived far outweigh the theoretical arguments that may be advanced.

SECTION 2. RULES FOR INTERPRETATION OF DISTRICT BOUNDARIES

Where uncertainty exists as to the boundaries of districts as shown on the Official Zoning Map, the following rules shall apply:

1. Boundaries indicated as approximately following the center lines of streets, highways, or alleys shall be construed to follow such center lines;

2. Boundaries indicated as approximately following platted lot lines shall be construed as following such lot lines;

3. Boundaries indicated as approximately following city limits shall be construed as following such city limits;

4. Boundaries indicated as following railroad lines shall be construed to be midway between the main tracks;

5. Boundaries indicated as following shore lines shall be construed to follow such shore lines, and in the event of change in the shore line shall be construed as moving with the actual shore line; boundaries indicated as approximately following the center lines of streams, rivers, canals, lakes, or other bodies of water shall be construed to follow such center lines;

6. Boundaries indicated as parallel to or extensions of features indicated in subsections 1 through 5 above shall be so construed. Distances not specifically indicated on the Official Zoning Map shall be determined by the scale of the map;

7. Where physical or cultural features existing on the ground are at variance with those shown on the Official Zoning Map, or in other circumstances not covered by subsections 1 through 6 above, the Board of Adjustment shall interpret the district boundaries.

8. Where a district boundary line divides a lot which was in single ownership at the time of passage of this ordinance, the Board of Adjustment may permit, as a special exception, the extension of the regulations for either portion of the lot not to exceed 50 feet beyond the district line into the remaining portion of the lot.

COMMENTARY—SECTION 2

The most careful and accurate drawing of the district boundary lines on the official zoning map will not eliminate completely the necessity for occasional interpretation of specifically where those lines fall on the ground itself. The possibility of disputes over the precise location of district boundary lines simply cannot be prevented. Errors in drawing the lines on the zoning map may occur. In larger municipalities, the scale of the map may have to be such, for example, that there is a question as to whether the boundary line runs down a back lot line or not. An issue of extension of a district boundary line can give rise to a dispute requiring interpretation.

For these reasons, every zoning ordinance should have a separate section setting out the rules to be followed when the question of the precise location of a district boundary line or segment thereof is raised. The model ordinance attempts to bring these rules for the interpretation of district boundaries together in one section. Far too many zoning ordinances have omitted these rules or scattered them at various places through the ordinance; thus an interested party has to search through the ordinance to find a rule that is applicable to his situation.

No particular comment is necessary on subsections 1–3. Subsection 4 is designed to apply whether there are one or several main railroad tracks along which a district boundary runs.

Subsection 5 is important where municipalities have lakes, canals, streams, bays, or ocean frontage within the city limits. Accretion, erosion, and man-made action of many types change the shore line; the first clause of subsection 5 provides for such possibilities. The word "change" has been deliberately used to include either man-made or natural change. The intent is to cover *all* forms of change. Actually, shore line sinuosities and their variable character can cause considerable problems in interpreting zoning district boundaries. The statement of subsection 5, we realize, is almost deceptively simple, but drafting any statement that would cover all eventualities is impossible. Subsection 5 is adequate for most purposes. Cities with complex waterways systems would want to give careful attention to changing the language of subsection 5, should they be adapting the model ordinance to their needs. Great care should be used, however, in altering the language.

Those municipalities with ocean frontage, or other water areas affected by the rise and fall of the tide might want to use some word other than "shore line," for the term does have a technical meaning in law. We caution against such change, however, without adequate legal advice. Generally, the term "shore line" will be found satisfactory.

The "center line" language is not uncommon, but again caution is necessary. Interpretations as to what constitutes the center line of a stream, for example, vary considerably from state to state and from time to time. Again, cities with extensive waterways will want to approach this problem with care.

Subsection 6 provides for the use of the parallel or the extension of the natural or man-made features used as district boundaries in subsections 1–5, when such parallel or extension is necessary for interpreting district boundaries. The scale of the official zoning map is declared to be the medium for the measurement of distance when distances are not specified on the map.

Man's best efforts will not prevent an occasional error from creeping into the zoning map. The error may be in drawing distict lines or it may be in the base map itself; such errors take many different forms. Some interpretative medium must be available, however, when the street or property layout existing on the ground is at variance with that shown on the official zoning map. If sound zoning policy and administration is followed, the correct instrument for affecting this interpretation will be the board of adjustment. Subsection 7 is drafted with the intent that the board of adjustment will perform this function. Such an intent is in line with the pertinent portions of the *Standard Act*, section 7.

In a sound zoning system, other than in connection with the granting of special exceptions, the board of adjustment will not act except on appeal from a decision of the official charged with the administration and enforcement of the zoning ordinance. Under subsection 7 of this section of the model text, the party concerned would apply to the official enforcing the zoning ordinance for a permit to take a particular action that depended upon a street or property layout at variance with the official zoning map. The administrative official would deny the permit saying, "This is the way it is on the map. I'm sorry, but I must deny your request. I have no administrative leeway in the matter." Thus rebuffed, the party concerned could then take an appeal to the board of adjustment, asking for an interpretation under the authority of subsection 7. The board could then make its decision, subject to section 7 of the *Standard Act* and section 9, subsection 1, of this model text.

It must be emphasized that in matters of this sort the administrative official charged with enforcing the ordinance should not, under good zoning administration, be allowed to make the interpretation. The intent of subsection 7 is to ensure that such matters are handled only by the board of adjustment.

Occasionally a district line may divide a lot. In such circumstances, provision should be made for boundary line adjustment without resorting to rezoning. Subsection 8 is designed to take care of such eventualities. The 50-foot figure in the draft is not, of course, at all sacred. Depending on circumstances found in particular communities, the figure might be increased or decreased.

SECTION 3. APPLICATION OF DISTRICT REGULATIONS

The regulations set by this ordinance within each district shall be minimum regulations and shall apply uniformly to each class or kind of structure or land, and particularly, except as hereinafter provided:

1. No building, structure, or land shall hereafter be used or occupied, and no building or structure or part thereof shall hereafter be erected, constructed, reconstructed, moved, or structurally altered except in conformity with all of the regulations herein specified for the district in which it is located.

2. No building or other structure shall hereafter be erected or altered:

   a) to exceed the height or bulk;

   b) to accommodate or house a greater number of families;

   c) to occupy a greater percentage of lot area;

   d) to have narrower or smaller rear yards, front yards, side yards, or other open spaces than herein required; or in any other manner contrary to the provisions of this ordinance.

3. No part of a yard, or other open space, or off-street parking or loading space required about or in connection with any building for the purpose of complying with this ordinance, shall be included as part of a yard, open space, or off-street parking or loading space similarly required for any other building.

4. No yard or lot existing at the time of passage of this ordinance shall be reduced in dimension or area below the minimum requirements set forth herein. Yards or lots created after the effective date of this ordinance shall meet at least the minimum requirements established by this ordinance.

5. All territory which may hereafter be annexed to the city shall be considered to be in the [here specify district, usually a single-family district] until otherwise classified.

COMMENTARY—SECTION 3

No model zoning text can include a meaningful schedule of district regulations. The commentary that follows section 5 of this model text explains why this is so and the role that a schedule of district regulations plays in the total picture of zoning law and administration. A zoning ordinance must, nevertheless, set out a textual background of intent and purpose dealing with how the schedule of district regulations, regardless of its substantive nature, is to be applied. This requirement is no less binding on the framers of a model text than it is on the drafters of an actual one.

The intent of section 3 of the model text is, by design, stated negatively and restrictively, to emphasize that the purpose of the schedule of district regulations is to prevent land from being used in any other way save in conformity with those regulations. The statements are essentially statements of policy, a declaration to those who live under the ordinance, those who administer and enforce it, and to the courts that may interpret it that the schedule of district regulations is a binding requirement and that it will be enforced.

Subsection 1 is a general statement declaring that lands, buildings, and structures are not to be used or occupied except in conformity with the schedule of district regulations and that buildings and structures cannot be constructed, moved, or altered except by meeting the terms of the regulations applicable to the district in which the activity will take place. The various terminology used in this subsection, some of it apparently synonymous in meaning, is designed to be broad enough to cover any and all possible shades and types of meanings in the broad area of "construction."

Subsection 2 sets out in list form, so that any person may know its contents at a glance, that the schedule of district regulations contains restrictions on the height and bulk of buildings; population density; relationship of size and structure to lot area; and front, side, and rear yard and open space sizes. (The word "bulk" must be included where a city regulates the minimum floor area of buildings.) As with most such listings, the subsection closes with the obvious, yet necessary, statement that buildings or other structures may not be erected in any other manner contrary to the ordinance. Citizens are on notice that the schedule of district regulations does say something about these various requirements and that it behooves an individual to check the ones appropriate to his district before drawing plans for his new home, grocery store, or apartment house.

Subsection 3 simply ensures that the requirements for yards, open spaces, off-street parking, or loading space will apply to each individual land parcel and that *one* parking space, meeting the requirements for one building on one parcel of land, will not be allowed to serve for *two* such buildings. The courts have generally held in recent years that cities can require that off-street parking and loading spaces be provided, even in residential areas. To make such provisions retroactive would be difficult, but in constructing a new shopping center, for example, the owners can be required to include adequate parking and loading facilities. Thus the schedule of district regulations can carry such requirements, varying the number of parking spaces or size of yard with the different districts.

Subsection 4 is a statement of intent and policy in regard to yards and lots. Those existing at the time of the enactment of the ordinance are not thereafter to be reduced in size below the minimums stated in the schedule of district regulations. All yards and lots created after the passage of the ordinance shall conform at least to the minimums stated in the schedule of district regulations where they are located. (Section 4 of the model text deals with non-conformities; yards or lots existing at the time of the adoption of the ordinance and below the minimums for the district in which they are located are protected under section 4.)

Whether specifically stated or not, the schedule of district regulations must meet the well-established legal test of uniform application within the particular district; nevertheless it is best to state the principle. Further, the model declares that the regulations in the districts shall be minimum regulations. The hope, seldom realized since minimums tend to become standards, is that individuals will, if possible, want to go beyond the stated district minimums. In addition, section 14 of the text of the model zoning ordinance reinforces this idea by declaring that any higher standards, those set in deed restrictions for example, shall apply over the minimum standards of the zoning ordinance and the schedule of district regulations.

The last paragraph of section 3 deals with a particularly tricky problem and one for which a perfect solution probably cannot be devised. Areas being annexed to a city *ought* to be zoned at the time of annexation, but usually they are not. Where annexation depends upon a favorable vote of the people in the area sought to be annexed, annexation may be defeated because of

announced zoning intentions. The matter is political dynamite in many cases.
Since the usual pattern of municipal annexation is that of adding a square
to a square, in the previous editions of this work we used phraseology which
zoned annexed territory "in the same manner as the contiguous territory in-
side previous city limits until otherwise classified." This language still might
prove more satisfactory for many cities than that now used in subsection 5.

But the earlier language offered special difficulties for cities with highly
irregular boundaries. Territory annexed in such circumstances could have
two, or more, "contiguous" zonings.

The language now used does have the advantage of definiteness, though we
resort to it reluctantly. Placing all newly annexed territory in a specific, even
though interim, classification can result in legal problems, especially if the
continguous area has been used for industrial or commercial purposes.

Where a city is so located as to be completely surrounded by land zoned
under a county resolution, a better solution might be to provide in the city
ordinance that newly annexed land would retain county zoning designations
until otherwise classified by the city. This solution, too, will offer problems in
some states, however, for the city would, during the interim period, in effect
be enforcing a county zoning resolution.

Certainly there is no perfect solution, but each zoning ordinance should
probably contain language on the point tailored to the city's particular situation. Halfway facetiously, it may be noted that bringing into a city territory
that ought to be in the city is such an extremely difficult problem in most
states that it makes the problem of "how to zone such territory" somewhat less
acute than it might be!

SECTION 4. NON-CONFORMING LOTS, NON-CONFORMING USES OF LAND, NON-CONFORMING STRUCTURES, NON-CONFORMING USES OF STRUCTURES AND PREMISES, AND NON-CONFORMING CHARACTERISTICS OF USE

1. *Intent.*—Within the districts established by this ordinance or
amendments that may later be adopted there exist

(*a*) lots,

(*b*) structures,

(*c*) uses of land and structures, and

(*d*) characteristics of use

which were lawful before this ordinance was passed or amended, but
which would be prohibited, regulated, or restricted under the terms
of this ordinance or future amendment. It is the intent of this ordinance
to permit these non-conformities to continue until they are removed,
but not to encourage their survival. It is further the intent of this

ordinance that non-conformities shall not be enlarged upon, expanded or extended, nor be used as grounds for adding other structures or uses prohibited elsewhere in the same district.

Non-conforming uses are declared by this ordinance to be incompatible with permitted uses in the districts involved. A non-conforming use of a structure, a non-conforming use of land, or a non-conforming use of structure and land in combination shall not be extended or enlarged after passage of this ordinance by attachment on a building or premises of additional signs intended to be seen from off the premises, or by the addition of other uses, of a nature which would be prohibited generally in the district involved.

To avoid undue hardship, nothing in this ordinance shall be deemed to require a change in the plans, construction, or designated use of any building on which actual construction was lawfully begun prior to the effective date of adoption or amendment of this ordinance and upon which actual building construction has been carried on diligently. Actual construction is hereby defined to include the placing of construction materials in permanent position and fastened in a permanent manner. Where excavation or demolition or removal of an existing building has been substantially begun preparatory to rebuilding, such excavation or demolition or removal shall be deemed to be actual construction, provided that work shall be carried on diligently.

2. *Non-Conforming Lots of Record.*—In any district in which single-family dwellings are permitted, a single-family dwelling and customary accessory buildings may be erected on any single lot of record at the effective date of adoption or amendment of this ordinance, notwithstanding limitations imposed by other provisions of this ordinance. Such lot must be in separate ownership and not of continuous frontage with other lots in the same ownership. This provision shall apply even though such lot fails to meet the requirements for area or width, or both, that are generally applicable in the district, provided that yard dimensions and requirements other than these applying to area or width, or both, of the lot shall conform to the regulations for the district in which such lot is located. Variance of yard requirements shall be obtained only through action of the Board of Adjustment.

If two or more lots or combinations of lots and portions of lots with continuous frontage in single ownership are of record at the time of passage or amendment of this ordinance, and if all or part of the lots do not meet the requirements established for lot width and area, the lands involved shall be considered to be an undivided parcel for the purposes of this ordinance, and no portion of said parcel shall be used or sold in a manner which diminishes compliance with lot width and area requirements established by this ordinance, nor shall any division of any parcel be made which creates a lot with width or area below the requirements stated in this ordinance.

3. *Non-Conforming Uses of Land (Or Land with Minor Structures Only).*—Where at the time of passage of this ordinance lawful use of land exists which would not be permitted by the regulations imposed by this ordinance, and where such use involves no individual structure with a replacement cost exceeding $1,000, the use may be continued so long as it remains otherwise lawful, provided:

a) No such non-conforming use shall be enlarged or increased, nor extended to occupy a greater area of land than was occupied at the effective date of adoption or amendment of this ordinance;

b) No such non-conforming use shall be moved in whole or in part to any portion of the lot or parcel other than that occupied by such use at the effective date of adoption or amendment of this ordinance;

c) If any such non-conforming use of land ceases for any reason for a period of more than 30 days, any subsequent use of such land shall conform to the regulations specified by this ordinance for the district in which such land is located.

d) No additional structure not conforming to the requirements of this ordinance shall be erected in connection with such non-conforming use of land.

4. *Non-Conforming Structures.*—Where a lawful structure exists at the effective date of adoption or amendment of this ordinance that could not be built under the terms of this ordinance by reason of restrictions on area, lot coverage, height, yards, its location on the lot, or other requirements concerning the structure, such structure may be continued so long as it remains otherwise lawful, subject to the following provisions:

a) No such non-conforming structure may be enlarged or altered in a way which increases its non-conformity, but any structure or portion thereof may be altered to decrease its non-conformity.

b) Should such non-conforming structure or non-conforming portion of structure be destroyed by any means to an extent of more than 50 per cent of its replacement cost at time of destruction, it shall not be reconstructed except in conformity with the provisions of this ordinance;

c) Should such structure be moved for any reason for any distance whatever, it shall thereafter conform to the regulations for the district in which it is located after it is moved.

5. *Non-Conforming Uses of Structures or of Structures and Premises in Combination.*—If lawful use involving individual structures with a replacement cost of $1,000 or more, or of structure and premises in combination, exists at the effective date of adoption or amendment of this ordinance, that would not be allowed in the district under the terms of this ordinance, the lawful use may be continued so long as it remains otherwise lawful, subject to the following provisions:

a) No existing structure devoted to a use not permitted by this ordinance in the district in which it is located shall be enlarged, extended, constructed, reconstructed, moved, or structurally altered except in changing the use of the structure to a use permitted in the district in which it is located;

b) Any non-conforming use may be extended throughout any parts of a building which were manifestly arranged or designed for such use at the time of adoption or amendment of this ordinance, but no such use shall be extended to occupy any land outside such building;

c) If no structural alterations are made, any non-conforming use of a structure, or structure and premises, may as a special exception be changed to another non-conforming use provided that the Board of Adjustment, either by general rule or by making findings in the specific case, shall find that the proposed use is equally appropriate or more appropriate to the district than the existing non-conforming use. In permitting such change, the Board of Adjustment may require appropriate conditions and safeguards in accord with the provisions of this ordinance;

d) Any structure, or structure and land in combination, in or on which a non-conforming use is superseded by a permitted use, shall thereafter conform to the regulations for the district, and the non-conforming use may not thereafter be resumed;

e) When a non-conforming use of a structure, or structure and premises in combination, is discontinued or abandoned for six consecutive months or for 18 months during any three-year period (except when government action impedes access to the premises), the structure, or structure and premises in combination, shall not thereafter be used except in conformity with the regulations of the district in which it is located;

f) Where non-conforming use status applies to a structure and premises in combination, removal or destruction of the structure shall eliminate the non-conforming status of the land. Destruction for the purpose of this subsection is defined as damage to an extent of more than 50 per cent [or other figure] of the replacement cost at time of destruction.

6. *Repairs and Maintenance.*—On any non-conforming structure or portion of a structure containing a non-conforming use, work may be done in any period of 12 consecutive months on ordinary repairs, or on repair or replacement of non-bearing walls, fixtures, wiring, or plumbing, to an extent not exceeding 10 per cent of the current replacement cost of the non-conforming structure or non-conforming portion of the structure as the case may be, provided that the cubic content existing when it became non-conforming shall not be increased.

If a non-conforming structure or portion of a structure containing a non-conforming use becomes physically unsafe or unlawful due to lack of repairs and maintenance, and is declared by any duly authorized official to be unsafe or unlawful by reason of physical condition, it shall not thereafter be restored, repaired, or rebuilt except in conformity with the regulations of the district in which it is located.

Nothing in this ordinance shall be deemed to prevent the strengthening or restoring to a safe condition of any building or part thereof declared to be unsafe by any official charged with protecting the public safety, upon order of such official.

7. *Uses Under Special Exception Provisions Not Non-Conforming Uses.*—Any use which is permitted as a special exception in a district

under the terms of this ordinance (other than a change through Board
of Adjustment action from a non-conforming use to another use not
generally permitted in the district) shall not be deemed a non-conforming use in such district, but shall without further action be considered
a conforming use.

COMMENTARY—SECTION 4

Zoning law and administration offer many difficult problems but few are
more vexing than the one of how to handle the problem of non-conformities.
No matter how carefully the district boundaries are drawn, certain lands,
buildings, or structures already in existence at the time the zoning ordinance
is adopted do not meet the district requirements as set out in the schedule of
district regulations. Under the law, these lands, buildings, or structures must
be allowed to remain or, under recent techniques, a reasonable time must be
allowed to bring them into conformity with the schedule of district regulations.

The root of some of the difficulty can be laid at least in part to the fact
that the drafters and administrators of zoning ordinances have not sorted
out in their own minds the various types of non-conformities. Too frequently,
perhaps, there has even been a failure to recognize that there are different
types of non-conformities. The term most frequently used in this area of zoning
law and administration has been "non-conforming use." A better approach
appears to be possible by utilizing the broader and inclusive term "non-
conformities," for non-conforming use is but one phase of the general classification of non-conformities. Thus there are non-conforming uses of land, non-
conforming uses of structures and premises, non-conforming characteristics
of use, non-conforming lots, and non-conforming structures.

Section 4 of the model text is premised on the concept that giving an
organizational pattern to what has previously been shuffled together will reduce considerably the problem of handling non-conformities. This approach
is relatively new and is found in only a few ordinances that are in existence
today.

Section 4 is premised, too, on our belief that the schedule of district regulations and boundaries of the districts, the heart of the zoning ordinance,
will be drawn only after much careful thought and analysis of pertinent materials, such as land use maps, growth maps, parcel maps, and similar items.
Since determination of district boundaries and establishment of the schedule
of district regulations is so vital to zoning legislation, the drafters will want
to avoid creating non-conforming uses in areas in which such uses are proper,
or in which they might be expanded without affecting the public interest.
Moreover, the principle is well established in law that the police power can
be used only where there is an infringement of the public interest; if a use
is such that it is impossible to demonstrate any deleterious effect on the public
interest, then it should not be barred from the district. There should be as
little disruption as possible of established local patterns.

If the schedule of district regulations and map are carefully drawn based on exhaustive data, non-conformities will not be numerous. For example, areas in which agricultural lands and uses are common should not be included in a district where agricultural uses are barred; including such land in agricultural use in a district where such uses are barred means they must be categorized as non-conforming. One measure of good drafting is that in preparing district boundaries and schedule of district regulations non-conformities are held to a minimum. Only in the very rare instance will a community be found where the pattern is such as to prevent accomplishing the aim.

The purpose of writing non-conformity provisions into the text of the zoning ordinance is to recognize that non-conformities must be allowed to continue (declaring that they must stop the day the ordinance is enacted would be unlawful) but that the municipality does not intend to encourage their permanent survival in any way. The existence of the non-conformities is not compatible with other characteristics of the district.

Intent. Subsection 1. Subsection 1 of section 4 of the model text states this intent clearly, and states it in terms of the various categories of non-conformities. This provision is a very important one. Generally, if non-conformities cease, whether by act of God, economic forces, or other cause, they may not be resumed. Not only will non-conformities not be encouraged but the existence of non-conformities is not allowable as grounds for the granting of variances for other properties by the board of adjustment. (See this model text, section 9, subsection 3 (*a*) and discussion thereon.)

The final paragraph of subsection 1 of section 4 is, in some respects, unnecessary. Where actual construction, including demolition or excavation precedent to erection, of a non-conforming structure is begun prior to the enactment of a zoning ordinance, such construction must, under law, be allowed to proceed to conclusion. Further the intended use of the building, even though the use be a non-conforming one, must be allowed. Were the city to attempt to halt such construction, a legal doctrine known as the doctrine of equitable estoppel could be invoked and the city could be enjoined from trying to halt such construction. The final paragraph of subsection 1 incorporates this legal principle.

Unlike some existing ordinances, however, the final paragraph of subsection 1 defines what is meant by actual construction and, of more importance, provides that the construction must be carried on diligently. Far too many cities have uncompleted structures on which no work has been done for years. If work on a non-conforming structure is not effectively and diligently carried on but has stopped and there is no evidence of intent to resume, there is no reason to allow forever the privilege of non-conforming status. (In this connection, reference should be made to the model text, section 7, subsections 2, 3, and 5 for general application of the principle of construction being carried on diligently.)

Non-Conforming Lots of Record. Subsection 2. The remaining materials of section 4 break down the non-conformities into their various categories. A non-conforming lot of record is, when one thinks about the matter, not a non-conforming use. There is a generally established legal principle that an individual must be allowed to do something with his lot. It may be too narrow to build a house and yet provide side yards specified for the district in the schedule of district regulations. The correct procedure under such circumstances is for the individual to apply for a building permit to the administrative official enforcing the ordinance. The official has no discretion in the matter and must deny the request. The individual then should take an appeal to the board of adjustment for a variance. The proper functions of the administrative official and the board of adjustment are thus preserved.

The first paragraph of subsection 2 of section 4 of the model text preserves these various legal and administrative principles by express language and by necessary relationship to other sections of the model text. There is, first of all, the explicit guarantee that a single family dwelling can be erected on any lot in a district where single family dwellings are permitted, providing the yard and other requirements *not* involving area or width are met. This meets the legal requirement that a man must be allowed to do something with his lot. Secondly, reference to the model text, section 9, subsections 1 and 3, and section 11 will show that the procedure outlined above should be followed.

Paragraph 2 of subsection 2 of section 4 represents an approach to the problem of what to do when lots on the original plat are extremely narrow, say 25 feet, but the schedule of district regulations provides for 50 or 75 foot minimum widths. Florida, especially among the 50 states, has a record of substandard subdivision development; developers laid out 25 or 40 foot width lots, not because they expected anybody to buy a single lot but because this gave the developers a sort of marginal approach. (This pattern, incidentally, continues today in a number of Florida counties, with advertisements reading in some cases "Minimum—two or three lots!") Caught with such a single lot in the middle of a block, the developer sold it, rather than lose his investment.

Such subdivision patterns far too often play a part in determining district regulations when zoning later comes along. The argument is that since the area is platted for 25 or 40 foot lots, the district regulations should be drafted with that minimum. This reasoning ignores actualities. The fact of the matter is that no city should attempt to draft a schedule of district regulations without a parcel map or ownership map at hand as well as the usual land use map. A parcel or ownership map will usually show, in the case of these substandard developments, that only a very few of the single narrow lots are in individual ownership; most owners have two or three adjoining lots. There are virtually no 25 or 40 foot ownerships. There is no excuse for allowing an individual to argue for an extraordinary or undesirable density (one of the reasons for zoning in the first place) merely because he happens to own a row of six lots, each 25 or 40 feet wide.

The model text provisions of section 4, subsection 2, paragraph 2, are not common but may lawfully be used. In effect, the undivided parcel of two or more lots cannot be divided, if as a parcel it is still below the minimum width set in the schedule of district regulations. Where division of a parcel is sought, each portion must meet the width and area requirements of the schedule of district regulations. The few single lots or the undivided parcel below width and area requirements are simply treated as non-conforming lots.

Most zoning ordinances do not establish minimum lot sizes in districts other than those in which single-family dwellings are permitted (*e.g.*, industrial districts). It is often desirable in industrial or commercial districts to establish varying minimum lot requirements for permitted uses. Where this is done, it is necessary to set forth certain uses (*e.g.*, offices or personal service establishments) for which no minimum lot is specified. Thus there would be no non-conforming lots, in the sense of a lot so small as to prohibit *all* uses, in a commercial or industrial district.

Non-Conforming Uses of Land (Or Land With Minor Structures Only). *Subsection 3.* Land alone may be used in a non-conforming way. Agricultural uses, for example, might have been established in an area where such uses are later prohibited under the schedule of district regulations. Careful drawing of district boundaries and the schedule of district regulations will, of course, make such a situation the exception rather than the rule.

The model text, section 4, subsection 3, recognizes the fact that land can be used in non-conforming fashion. Requirements are set out, in order that the use will not be extended, enlarged, or moved. Should the non-conforming use of the land cease, the use may not later be resumed, but all uses shall then be conforming ones.

Smaller cities, particularly, may be faced with the problem of non-conforming use of land for agricultural purposes. The intent of this section is to include agricultural pursuits where they are non-conforming. Lands lying fallow are considered to be in agricultural use and in non-conforming use if agriculture is prohibited in the district by the schedule of district regulations.

Because considerably less investment is involved in the use of land alone, this subsection on non-conforming use of land is considerably tighter than the provisions of subsection 5 dealing with non-conforming uses of structures or structures and premises in combination. The provision concerning incidental or minor structures with individual replacement costs not exceeding $1,000 is intended to avert problems that might be raised by the existence of a shed or shack on the premises. Most lands do have *some* structures, and this provision reaches one or several cheap structures. The $1,000 figure may be lowered or raised, depending on circumstances, but it should be remembered that if the figure is too high the question of unlawful confiscation might be raised.

Non-Conforming Structures, Subsection 4. The *use* of a structure built prior to the adoption of a zoning ordinance may conform completely to the schedule of district regulations. To take an example, a house built prior to the enactment of the ordinance might have a bedroom or carport in what is now a required side yard. Section 4, subsection 4, of the model text is de-

signed to cover this type of non-conformity. Again the intent is that the structure shall not be enlarged or altered, except if such alteration or change
brings it into conformity with district regulations. Moving the structure is
possible only if after the moving the structure conforms.

The word "structure" is deliberately used in section 4, subsection 4, and
elsewhere throughout the model text to include "anything constructed or
erected with a fixed location on the ground, or attached to something having
a fixed location on the ground." Thus the term includes, among other things,
buildings, walls, fences, billboards, and poster panels (see section 18 of the
model text, "Definitions"). A "structure" in the meaning of the model text
is most definitely not limited to buildings.

It is customary in zoning to allow replacement or partial replacement of
structures destroyed through acts of God such as fire or hurricane. The model
text sets a figure of 50 per cent of replacement cost as the cut-off point of
destruction. Destruction of less than 50 per cent of replacement cost is re-
pairable in non-conforming fashion; destruction of greater than that amount
requires reconstruction in conformity with the schedule of district regulations.

There is no particular magic in the figure 50 per cent. A higher figure, say
60 or 75 per cent, can be used if the policy decision is taken to treat such
non-conformities more leniently. The 50 per cent figure is a tighter figure.
Replacement cost is used because it is relatively easy to determine and because assessed valuation figures for tax purposes are not always realistic.

*Non-Conforming Uses of Structures or of Structures and Premises in Com-
bination. Subsection 5.* Subsection 5 of section 4 of the model ordinance is
concerned with what to many people appears to constitute the sum of non-
conformities. Again the intent is that such non-conforming uses of structures
shall not be enlarged and that the ultimate purpose is to make the uses of
such buildings, whenever lawfully possible, conforming uses.

The caution noted earlier in this discussion bears repetition. Unless fric-
tion, actual or potential, exists between a use and the district in which it is
located, such use should not be non-conforming. Unless a use is adverse to
the public interest, it should not be categorized as a non-conforming use. If,
for example, the judgment of the drafters of an ordinance is that home occupations probably should be allowed in a district, these occupations should
be included in the schedule of district regulations as customary uses allowable in such districts. They should not under these circumstances be placed
in the category of non-conforming uses.

Paragraph (c) of this subsection utilizes the special exception (see pages
55–57 for a discussion of the special exception) as the instrument whereby
changes in non-conforming uses may be made under certain circumstances.
Under this provision, "up-grading" of non-conforming uses is possible. Further, unlike the variance, the applicant for a special exception does not need
to demonstrate hardship.

Paragraph (e) of this subsection contains a provision designed to protect
those persons who must for a time discontinue their non-conforming use

through no fault of their own. Governmental action, like the widening of a road, frequently will last over a good many months. It would not be fair to utilize the discontinuance provisions under such circumstances, so an exception is included.

Comment has been made, in connection with the discussion of subsection 4, concerning destruction of non-conforming structures; these comments apply to paragraph (*f*) of this subsection.

Repairs and Maintenance. Subsection 6. Repairs and maintenance on buildings that are non-conforming are necessary as with other buildings that do conform. Section 4, subsection 6, of the model text covers the manner and requirement for making such repairs. The 10 per cent figure of the first paragraph is provided to cover the normal upkeep type maintenance plus minor alterations and modernization not changing the cubic content of the building.

The second paragraph of this subsection is designed to reinforce a minimum housing code, if the city has one, or to provide some small leverage for eliminating certain unsafe buildings if the city does not have a minimum housing code. The regulation is limited to those buildings that become unsafe *due to lack of repairs and maintenance.* These buildings, *where they are used for non-conforming purposes,* may not be restored or rebuilt except in conformity with the zoning ordinance.

Uses Under Special Exception Provisions Not Non-Conforming Uses. Subsection 7. Many persons, including members of boards of adjustment and individuals charged with various aspects of zoning administration, do not understand the distinction between a special exception and a variance. Each of these terms is defined and discussed later (see the model text, section 9, subsections 2 and 3, and the commentary thereon). The purpose of subsection 7 of section 4 of the model text is to ensure that uses authorized under special exception provisions are classified as *conforming* uses; uses authorized under special exceptions are not subject to the requirements of section 4. It should be noted, too, that a use of land, existing prior to the adoption of the ordinance, that would be a special exception under the ordinance is, without further action, conforming under these provisions.

A Few General Words. We would call attention to some problems that arise in connection with non-conformities.

The first deals with the valuation of property. Wherever there are issues of repair or damage of non-conforming structures, the obvious question arises: "What value shall be used in applying the provisions on non-conformities?" Should one speak of assessed value, replacement value, or sales value at the time the damage occurred? Or should some other value, perhaps a combination of one or more of those just listed, be used? Destruction of a building to 50 per cent of "value" alone is impossible to determine. Some adjective must be used. Sales value is too nebulous, and varying assessment practices often make assessed value unrealistic. If the assessed valuations are realistic, that figure would be easier to use, for such values are a matter of public record. Replacement value certainly is not an exact measurement, but in the context of a zoning ordinance, it is probably the best type of figure that can be used. Replacement value can usually be established by the people in the vicinity, either by contractors or by appraisers.

A second question deals with a matter of technique to which increasing attention is being given. The intent of provisions on non-conformities, it was stated at the outset of this discussion, is to allow them to continue but not to encourage their survival. A number of cities have shown interest in methods for compelling the *removal* of non-conformities through establishing amortization schedules for various types of non-conformities.

Statutes designed to enforce the elimination or termination of such uses have been found valid in a number of states (see RHYNE, MUNICIPAL LAW [1957], 922–24, and YOKELEY, ZONING LAW AND PRACTICE [1965], section 16–14, for a discussion of the point raised here and citations to cases). Such statutes must, of course, be reasonably related to the exercise of the police power; most definitely they cannot require a termination of the use without giving sufficient notice. It is at this point that the concept of amortizing the investment is a useful one. At the conclusion of a prescribed period, the use can no longer be continued. In most jurisdictions, though the point is open to some argument, non-conforming uses can be eliminated if the amortization base period is a reasonable one.

In actual operation, the amortization base period is first established. In applying that period to a structure, the date used as a base point is the date when the structure was erected. Take, for instance, a concrete block building erected in 1940. The amortization period for such structures set out in a 1950 zoning ordinance is, let us say, 30 years. The termination date is 1970.

The technique has attracted considerable interest. In cases of open air uses not involving structures, the base period can be relatively short. Uses involving structures with considerable value require longer base periods. This relatively new way of handling non-conforming uses offers great promise.

We did not choose to include provisions in the model text setting up base period schedules. There is, to begin with, a serious question as to whether any given community will want to resort to what substantial elements of the area will view as "radical" measures. There is, further, no general agreement yet as to what constitutes "proper" amortization bases. The appellate court cases are not yet sufficiently numerous to work out a complete rationale. Examination of zoning ordinances including this feature discloses a wide variation of judgment as to what is "reasonable." The principle is sound. More, not less, resort will be had to it in the future.

Increased road construction activity has focused attention on a third problem. There are many instances where legitimate, non-conforming use of land has been penalized unfairly by road widening activity (or, indeed, by government taking of land for other purposes). Frequently there is sufficient depth to the land parcel to permit the reconstruction of the non-conforming use or to permit an addition to the use of equal building bulk to that which has been necessitated by the government taking.

Some cities may wish to adopt provisions granting permission as of right, or as a special exception, to reconstruct a non-conforming use *on the same parcel of land* where the destruction of the non-conforming use was the result of government taking. Adoption of such a provision would be a matter of particular city policy.

No legal requirement forces a city to adopt such language. Clearly there is no doubt that such a provision is a weakening of the principle that non-conformities should not be encouraged to continue. Certainly reconstruction of the use should not be permitted on another parcel of land, but consideration of the totality of circumstances combined with known future plans for street widening and other construction activities by government might dictate such a requirement.

SECTION 5. SCHEDULE OF DISTRICT REGULATIONS ADOPTED

District regulations shall be as set forth in the Schedule of District Regulations, hereby adopted by reference and declared to be a part of this ordinance, and in Section 6 of this ordinance, entitled "Supplementary District Regulations."

COMMENTARY—SECTION 5

In publishing this model text of a zoning ordinance, we have expressed our belief that the text of an ordinance can be drafted and standardized to a considerable degree. The schedule of district regulations cannot be so standardized. Variations in local conditions are too great; imposition of a standardized schedule of district regulations on a community would result only in increasing the problems in land use control rather than in decreasing them. (In the appendix, pages 93–98, some suggestions on drafting a schedule of district regulations are offered.)

The final product, the zoning ordinance, stands or falls on the soundness of the district boundaries and the schedule of district regulations. Outside consultants can *help* in this phase of the work, particularly in the organizational aspects, but only the efforts and attention of local citizens can ensure that the district boundaries and the schedule of district regulations really fit the needs of the individual community. The point deserves emphasis, for too many people tend to assume that the outside zoning and planning consultant is the answer to all needs and problems and that no special effort on the part of the citizens of the municipality is necessary. A less correct appraisal of the situation can scarcely be imagined.

We follow the best approved drafting practice in providing that the official zoning map and the schedule of district regulations shall be a part of the ordinance, adopted by reference. They are *not* part of the *text* of the ordinance. Use of the method of adoption by reference gives much greater drafting flexibility with no loss whatsoever in the legal status of the final product. Use of such a method greatly eases, too, the problem facing the average citizen as he attempts to find out just what the limitations are.

It is in the schedule of district regulations, customarily set up in columns, that the various requirements for specific districts are detailed. Only such items as vary from district to district appear on the schedule; it does not contain general material. Here one should find columns listing requirements for such matters as lot size, yards, building heights and bulk, population density, permitted uses, percentage of allowable lot space which may be used for building, accessory uses, special exceptions permitted, prohibited uses, signs, and other matters. The list is intended to be illustrative only, but it shows the types of things normally specified in schedules of district regulations.

As an aid in establishing a framework for preparing a schedule of district regulations, we have included in the appendix suggested column heads and a short discussion of the techniques involved.

SECTION 6. SUPPLEMENTARY DISTRICT REGULATIONS

1. *Visibility at Intersections in Residential Districts.*—On a corner lot in any residential district, nothing shall be erected, placed, planted, or allowed to grow in such a manner as materially to impede vision between a height of two and a half and ten feet above the centerline grades of the intersecting streets in the area bounded by the street lines of such corner lots and a line joining points along said street lines 50 feet from the point of the intersection.

2. *Fences, Walls, and Hedges.*—Notwithstanding other provisions of this ordinance, fences, walls, and hedges may be permitted in any required yard, or along the edge of any yard, provided that no fence, wall, or hedge along the sides or front edge of any front yard shall be over two and one-half feet in height.

3. *Accessory Buildings.*—No accessory building shall be erected in any required yard, and no separate accessory building shall be erected within five feet of any other building.

4. *Erection of More than One Principal Structure on a Lot.*—In any district, more than one structure housing a permitted or permissible principal use may be erected on a single lot, provided that yard and other requirements of this ordinance shall be met for each structure as though it were on an individual lot.

5. *Exceptions to Height Regulations.*—The height limitations contained in the Schedule of District Regulations do not apply to spires, belfries, cupolas, antennas, water tanks, ventilators, chimneys, or other appurtenances usually required to be placed above the roof level and not intended for human occupancy.

6. *Structures To Have Access.*—Every building hereafter erected or moved shall be on a lot adjacent to a public street, or with access to an approved private street, and all structures shall be so located on lots as to provide safe and convenient access for servicing, fire protection, and required off-street parking.

7. *Parking, Storage, or Use of Major Recreational Equipment.*— For purposes of these regulations, major recreational equipment is defined as including boats and boat trailers, travel trailers, pick-up campers or coaches (designed to be mounted on automotive vehicles), motorized dwellings, tent trailers, and the like, and cases or boxes used for transporting recreational equipment, whether occupied by such equipment or not. No major recreational equipment shall be parked or stored on any lot in a residential district except in a car port or enclosed building or behind the nearest portion of a building to a street, provided however that such equipment may be parked anywhere on residential premises for not to exceed 24 hours during loading or unloading. No such equipment shall be used for living, sleeping, or housekeeping purposes when parked or stored on a residential lot, or in any location not approved for such use.

8. *Parking and Storage of Certain Vehicles.*—Automotive vehicles or trailers of any kind or type without current license plates shall not be parked or stored on any residentially zoned property other than in completely enclosed buildings.

COMMENTARY—SECTION 6

The proper location for detailed requirements and limitations for individual zoning districts is in the schedule of district regulations. A supplementary district regulation section, a part of the text of the ordinance, is necessary to take care of miscellaneous and left over material that may not apply in all districts but that may apply in groups of districts. In the theory of drafting good zoning legislation, the supplementary regulations section should not cover anything that applies universally throughout the city; the supplementary section should rather cover things that are applicable to several districts.

Section 6 of the model text for the most part contains material primarily applicable to residential districts. Subsection 1 is concerned with visibility at intersections in residential districts. Hedges and fences that are too high are the most grievous offenders of public safety in this regard but uncontrolled structures and buildings can also cause difficulty. The 2½-foot requirement is practical and, from the safety standpoint, the maximum that should be allowed. Drivers of small European sports cars coming up to an intersection where the hedge is more than 2½ feet above the center grade line of the street simply cannot see over it. Most children can be seen over a 2½ foot hedge or solid fence. If the limit is raised to 3 or 4 feet, the requirement might just as well be omitted. Allowing obstructions above 10 feet is necessary because of tree limbs; such an obstruction in no way affects safety factors.

A good case can be made that the material of subsection 1 simply should not be in a zoning ordinance. Cities should have ordinances prohibiting obstructions to visibility at intersections in residential areas. If a city has a sound ordinance on this point, and is enforcing it, then subsection 1 may be omitted. We have included the language because so few cities have legislation dealing with this safety hazard.

The intent of subsection 2 is to allow higher fences and hedges in side and rear yards. The maximum of 2½ feet for front yard fences or hedges is preserved as a safety factor, particularly where small children are concerned. Some cities include maximum height provisions on side and rear yard fences. The matter is one of policy for the individual city. No attempt has been made here to say how high side or rear yard fences should be. Good fences make good neighbors until attempts are made by ordinance to restrict height or type of fence! This relatively unimportant topic can be the subject of immense controversy.

Subsection 3 is necessary in order to prevent the erection of accessory buildings in required yards. Without such a restriction, accessory buildings will be erected in required yards and the purpose for having yards will be effectively negated.

Subsection 4 makes it clear that, if the parcel of land is large enough to meet requirements, more than one principal structure may be placed on a "lot." There is no reason to penalize owners of large parcels.

Modern living requires that some structures be higher than height limitations would normally permit. Structures like television antennas and chimneys might just as well be covered by providing for them in the ordinance, rather than requiring board of adjustment action or "looking the other way" and not enforcing the ordinance. Subsection 5 deals with this problem. Note that the exception to height regulations specifically does not permit such exceptions where the structure is designed for human habitation.

Subsection 6 is necessary to meet a most difficult problem so far as most cities are concerned. Some ordinances provide that all buildings must front on a public street. The provision is designed to bolster weaknesses in subdivision regulations and to keep the city from having to assume unnecessary street maintenance costs. Requiring frontage on a public street, and thereby access, is very much favored by us in those circumstances where the provision is practical and legally supportable.

Such language is, however, of doubtful validity in some states, so we have chosen, for model text purposes, to include "approved private street" language as well. Erection of buildings without adequate access should not be permitted. One home at the end of a mile easement offers no particular problems, but 30 homes on such an easement inevitably (because of the votes involved!) leads to the assumption of street improvement and maintenance by the city, with resulting costs to *all* the taxpayers. Lack of access, moreover, offers health, policing, and fire problems.

As the American people become increasingly recreation-minded, problems grow as to the parking of bulky items of equipment like camp trailers. Individual cities may want to vary the requirements of subsection 7, or eliminate it altogether. The language is offered as an example of what *may* be done. We have written some ordinances where parking of such vehicles was prohibited in front yards, or in front and side yards. One of us has written one ordinance which flatly prohibited such parking except in a completely enclosed structure; the town was a small, very highgrade, residential one.

Subsection 8 is a handy device for eliminating at least some of the "junk car" problem. Requirement of current license plate has proved a handy device for getting rid of the one or two junked cars that sometimes plague an otherwise satisfactory residential neighborhood.

SECTION 7. ADMINISTRATION AND ENFORCEMENT—
BUILDING PERMITS AND CERTIFICATES OF ZONING COMPLIANCE

1. *Administration and Enforcement.*—An administrative official designated by the [city council, city commission, city manager] shall administer and enforce this ordinance. He may be provided with the assistance of such other persons as the [city council, city commission, city manager] may direct.

If the administrative official shall find that any of the provisions of this ordinance are being violated, he shall notify in writing the person responsible for such violations, indicating the nature of the violation and ordering the action necessary to correct it. He shall order discontinuance of illegal use of land, buildings, or structures; removal of illegal buildings or structures or of illegal additions, alterations, or structural changes; discontinuance of any illegal work being done; or shall take any other action authorized by this ordinance to ensure compliance with or to prevent violation of its provisions.

2. *Building Permits Required.*—No building or other structure shall be erected, moved, added to, or structurally altered without a permit therefor, issued by the administrative official. No building permit shall be issued by the administrative official except in conformity with the provisions of this ordinance, unless he receives a written order from

the Board of Adjustment in the form of an administrative review, special exception, or variance as provided by this ordinance.

3. *Application for Building Permit.*—All applications for building permits shall be accompanied by plans in triplicate drawn to scale, showing the actual dimensions and shape of the lot to be built upon; the exact sizes and locations on the lot of buildings already existing, if any; and the location and dimensions of the proposed building or alteration. The application shall include such other information as lawfully may be required by the administrative official, including existing or proposed building or alteration; existing or proposed uses of the building and land; the number of families, housekeeping units, or rental units the building is designed to accommodate; conditions existing on the lot; and such other matters as may be necessary to determine conformance with, and provide for the enforcement of, this ordinance.

One copy of the plans shall be returned to the applicant by the administrative official, after he shall have marked such copy either as approved or disapproved and attested to same by his signature on such copy. The original and one copy of the plans, similarly marked, shall be retained by the administrative official.

4. *Certificates of Zoning Compliance for New, Altered, or Non-Conforming Uses.*—It shall be unlawful to use or occupy or permit the use or occupancy of any building or premises, or both, or part thereof hereafter created, erected, changed, converted, or wholly or partly altered or enlarged in its use or structure until a certificate of zoning compliance shall have been issued therefor by the administrative official stating that the proposed use of the building or land conforms to the requirements of this ordinance.

No non-conforming structure or use shall be maintained, renewed, changed, or extended until a certificate of zoning compliance shall have been issued by the administrative official. The certificate of zoning compliance shall state specifically wherein the non-conforming use differs from the provisions of this ordinance, provided that upon enactment or amendment of this ordinance, owners or occupants of non-conforming uses or structures shall have three months to apply for certificates of zoning compliance. Failure to make such application within three months shall be presumptive evidence that the property was in conforming use at the time of enactment or amendment of this ordinance.

No permit for erection, alteration, moving, or repair of any building shall be issued until an application has been made for a certificate of zoning compliance, and the certificate shall be issued in conformity with the provisions of this ordinance upon completion of the work.

A temporary certificate of zoning compliance may be issued by the administrative official for a period not exceeding six months during alterations or partial occupancy of a building pending its completion, provided that such temporary certificate may include such conditions and safeguards as will protect the safety of the occupants and the public.

The administrative official shall maintain a record of all certificates of zoning compliance, and a copy shall be furnished upon request to any person.

Failure to obtain a certificate of zoning compliance shall be a violation of this ordinance and punishable under Section 16 of this ordinance.

5. *Expiration of Building Permit.*—If the work described in any building permit has not begun within 90 days from the date of issuance thereof, said permit shall expire; it shall be cancelled by the administrative official; and written notice thereof shall be given to the persons affected.

If the work described in any building permit has not been substantially completed within two years of the date of issuance thereof, said permit shall expire and be cancelled by the administrative official, and written notice thereof shall be given to the persons affected, together with notice that further work as described in the cancelled permit shall not proceed unless and until a new building permit has been obtained.

6. *Construction and Use To Be as Provided in Applications, Plans, Permits, and Certificates of Zoning Compliance.*—Building permits or certificates of zoning compliance issued on the basis of plans and applications approved by the administrative official authorize only the use, arrangement, and construction set forth in such approved plans and applications, and no other use, arrangement, or construction. Use, arrangement, or construction at variance with that authorized shall be deemed violation of this ordinance, and punishable as provided by Section 16 hereof.

COMMENTARY—SECTION 7

Zoning ordinances require administration and enforcement. An outstanding ordinance can be spoiled by poor administration and enforcement; a poor ordinance may be a reasonably effective instrument with good administration and enforcement; a first class ordinance with top-notch administration and enforcement constitutes a practically unbeatable combination.

One great source of confusion in zoning law and administration arises from a lack of understanding of the proper role of the various instruments that play a part. There must be, first of all, an official of the city government, and such assistants as may be necessary, charged with the administration and enforcement of the ordinance. There must be an interpretive and safety valve mechanism, an instrument to which appeals can be taken, if a party deems it necessary; this instrument under section 7 of the *Standard Act* is the board of adjustment. Further recourse from the board of adjustment should lie only to the courts. The role of the city governing body is essentially a passive one, consisting primarily of passing or rejecting amendments to the ordinance. The city governing body plays an important extralegal part, too, in influencing community attitude toward zoning and planning.

The role of these instruments of zoning administration will be discussed at the appropriate point in the commentaries on the sections of the model text that follow. Section 7 of the model text is concerned with duties of the administrative official enforcing the ordinance and with the utilization of building permits and certificates of zoning compliance as administrative and enforcing tools.

Administration and Enforcement. Subsection 1. Efficient administration requires that a single person be given power and authority to accomplish the task set out. Responsibility for success or failure, for lax enforcement or for poor administration, can thus be determined. Good zoning administration requires that a single person be charged with the responsibility of administering and enforcing the ordinance. In subsection 1 of section 7 of the model text this person is denominated as the "administrative official."

Those who have become accustomed to calling the person administering and enforcing the zoning ordinance a "building inspector" may find the language of the model text a bit confusing at first. The practice of giving one official several different types of functions to perform is extremely common in small cities, where the building inspector, for example, serves not only as an inspector of construction activities but is given administrative duties in the zoning field as well. Differences among cities in nomenclature have led us to use the term "administrative official" to denote the official in charge of administration and enforcement of the ordinance. This is the language, too, of the *Standard Act.* Since the power to make appointments is lodged in different hands in different cities, the title of the proper appointing authority will have to be included in any adaptation of the model text.

Duties of the administrative official under subsection 1 and other pertinent portions of the ordinance and the legal standards provided for his guidance in this and other sections of the ordinance are clear: he receives applications of various types, inspects premises, checks and passes on building plans to see they meet zoning ordinance requirements, issues certificates of zoning compliance, takes specified actions when he uncovers violations of the ordinance, and orders discontinuance of illegal uses or illegal work in progress. He is not a judicial officer and exercises no quasi-judicial authority. He does not issue special exceptions or variances. His discretion is bounded carefully by the ordinance, and he has no authority to mitigate the severity of the application of the ordinance to individuals. Appeals lie from his decision only to the board of adjustment. The city governing body has no authority to overrule his decision or order that he grant a specific permit or take a particular action, except indirectly by amending the ordinance.

Such is the role of the administrative official under the terms of the model text. This conception of his role squares precisely with the terms of section 7 of the *Standard Act*. The fact that some cities have allowed the administrative official's role to expand to the point where he exercises some quasi-judicial power, or that city governing bodies sometimes have ordered him to take particular actions, does not justify further continuation of these and similar practices that are so antithetical to sound zoning law and practice.

Building Permits Required. Subsection 2. One of the prime tools of zoning administration and enforcement is the building permit. The building permit itself goes beyond the zoning framework; it extends, for example, to such items as plumbing and electrical inspection. The basic authority of the building permit is, or ought to be, the municipal building, plumbing, and electrical codes. But the application for the building permit is the "tip-off" that something is about to happen that will relate to the zoning ordinance. Requiring the administrative official to check and pass on applications for building permits to see whether or not the proposed construction meets the requirements of the ordinance is one effective method of enforcing zoning. In a small town where the building inspector (who administers and enforces the building code) and the administrative official (who administers and enforces the zoning ordinance) are the same person, the administrative processes involved are simplified. In larger towns, where two different persons handle these functions, separate authorizations should come from two officials or their designated subordinates before the building permit is issued. The administrative official enforcing the zoning ordinance is interested only in the zoning ramifications of the building permit applications.

The *Standard Act* says nothing about building permits or certificates of zoning compliance, but cities are authorized under it to enforce zoning and this is sufficient to cover the matter. The courts have held that requiring approval of the appropriate zoning authority prior to the issuance of a building permit is a proper exercise of municipal power.

Careful notice should be taken of the fact that the check for zoning compliance that is made on the application for a building permit involves ordinarily, *but certainly not exclusively,* mechanical questions. Have the proper front, side, and rear yards been provided? Are the requirements for percentage of lot that may be built on met? Naturally, it is to be presumed that approval would not be given to an application for a building permit to erect a filling station in a residential district where that type of use is excluded, but the normal emphasis in checking the building permit application for zoning conformity is rather more likely to be somewhat mechanical.

If the administrative official finds he cannot approve the issuance of the building permit because of the requirements of the ordinance, the applicant's correct appeal is to the board of adjustment. Perhaps, for example, the applicant may be entitled to a variance for a side yard of lesser width than that provided in the schedule of district regulations. Should such a variance be proper, the board then issues the necessary variance and order to the administrative official who must then approve, from the zoning standpoint, the granting of the building permit.

The intent of subsection 2 is to bring checking and passing on building permit applications within this frame of reference.

Application for Building Permit. Subsection 3. Using the requirement of zoning authority approval before the issuance of a building permit necessarily implies that such applications will have to contain materials pertaining to zoning. Such materials will be in addition to those required to determine whether or not the application meets the terms of the building code.

Subsection 3 of section 7 is designed to outline the types of information that the administrative official *may* require as well as the types of documents that *must* be supplied. Note should be taken that such information extends beyond mechanical data and includes material on the proposed use. For the purpose of establishing required yard lines, some cities may want to add to the zoning ordinance a requirement that a survey letter, dated within six months or so of the building permit application, be filed with the application.

In order that the applicant will be able to know the precise disposition made of the application by the administrative official, provision is made for the return of one set of plans to the applicant with the notation of action and the signature of the administrative official attesting such action.

Certificates of Zoning Compliance for New, Altered, or Non-Conforming Uses. Subsection 4. Few cities have taken stringent action against non-conformities or to prevent non-conformities, even though stringent action may be called for and, if handled reasonably, is legal. In some municipalities, persons have even started businesses in residential areas where they are clearly prohibited, doing so without bothering about permits. Within a few years, changes in city government personnel have made it impossible to check the origin and source of such non-conformities; no one really knows except the owner (and he never tells!) whether the business is a legitimately non-conforming one or not.

The requirement of a certificate of zoning compliance is designed to meet this and other types of problems. The major characteristic of the certificate of zoning compliance is that it *relates primarily to use,* although a non-conforming structure will also need a certificate of zoning compliance. (This requirement is to inhibit illegal additions to structures.) A non-conforming lot does not require a certificate of zoning compliance for it is not used or occupied; it is simply a vacant lot. An *old* use, that is, one in existence at the time of the adoption of the ordinance, *that is conforming in the district* in which it is located does not need a certificate of zoning compliance.

The certificate of zoning compliance relates *only* to zoning, and is suggested as a substitute for the "certificate of occupancy" frequently mentioned in *zoning* ordinances. Since a "certificate of occupancy" is required under *building codes,* dual use of the term is likely to lead to confusion. As a practical matter, the certificate of zoning compliance might well be entered on the certificate of occupancy issued in connection with the enforcement of building codes. The legal authority to require a certificate of zoning compliance appears clear.

At the time the zoning ordinance is passed, "new" uses automatically come into being. Old uses, if they continue and are conforming, are not affected. Building a house on a vacant lot in a residential district *after* the passage of the ordinance is a new use of the lot. Tearing down a small office building and erecting a grocery store, granted both the previous use and the new use are conforming, is an altered use. The purpose of the certificate of zoning compliance is to ensure that the new or altered use is a conforming one and, of almost equal importance, to have an adequate record on the point. In this sense, this particular type of use of the certificate of zoning compliance parallels the approval required on the building permit applications.

But the certificate of zoning compliance has another and very important function to fill in the scheme of zoning administration under the model text. It is an effective instrument in keeping track of non-conformities. The intent of this subsection, particularly as found in paragraph 2, is to place on record all of the non-conforming uses lawfully in existence at the time of the adoption of the ordinance. An owner or operator of a non-conforming use must apply for his certificate of zoning compliance within three months of the effective date of the ordinance; if his non-conforming use is otherwise lawful, he will be granted his certificate of zoning compliance. Though the use remains non-conforming, the owner or operator has now complied with the zoning ordinance. Possession of the certificate establishes a presumption that the use was a legitimate one at the time the non-conformity was acquired.

The non-conforming use is now a matter of public record; no future confusion can exist as to the exact nature and extent of the use. Any extension, change, or alteration of the non-conforming use, except by procedures outlined in the ordinance, can be immediately checked. In policing non-conformities, correct and accurate records are absolutely essential.

Failure to apply for a certificate of zoning compliance for a non-conforming use within the prescribed period is declared to establish a presumption that the use was a conforming one at the time of the adoption of the ordinance.

Continuance of the non-conforming use under such circumstances would subject the owner or operator to the penalties of the ordinance.

The burden of applying for certificates of zoning compliance for non-conforming uses is placed on the owner or operator under the model text. As authors of the model text we gave some thought to the inclusion of provisions requiring the administrative official, within a set period of time after the adoption of the ordinance, to send written notices to all persons operating non-conforming uses. Within a further period of time, such persons would have to apply for certificates of zoning compliance or the presumption would be made that the use was a conforming one, with the consequent possibility of imposition of penalties if the non-conforming use continued.

Placing such a requirement on the administrative officer would constitute no great burden for him in the average small- or medium-sized town, *if* the zoning ordinance has been drafted only after adequate data has been collected. If the ordinance is drawn on the basis of sufficient land use analysis, the administrative official will already have in his possession the location of all non-conforming uses. If the boundaries of the zoning districts are carefully framed, ordinarily there will not be very many non-conformities in each district. Sending out the proper notices should be no large chore.

Cities contemplating the use of the model text might consider including such a provision in the zoning ordinance. The suggestion shifts the burden from the owner or operator to the administrative official. Requiring notice might buttress the legality of this method of employing the certificate of zoning compliance. In the alternative, the city council might want to prescribe the requirement as a part of the administrative regulations set up to guide the conduct of the administrative official.

Placing the certificate of zoning compliance in the ordinance, as we have done, and then failing to administer and enforce it will, of course, accomplish nothing. Properly administered and enforced, it can be an invaluable aid in policing non-conformities. It is an instrument for providing invaluable records of an important phase of zoning activity, and the ultimate sanction of penalties is available to enforce it.

Expiration of Building Permit. Subsection 5. If the provisions of subsection 5 were found in all building codes, and enforced, there would be little reason for including it as a part of this model text. The provisions are designed to ensure that construction work will begin and that it will be diligently carried on. The intent is to prevent the extension of construction work over a period of years, the authority for such work being the original building permit.

Construction and Use To Be as Provided in Applications, Plans, Permits and Certificates of Zoning Compliance. Subsection 6. In many ways, this subsection merely restates the obvious, yet it is an important restatement. A building permit issued for the addition of a "guest room" to a house in a single-family residential district does *not* authorize the later renting of that room in violation of the zoning ordinance. Other examples, and they are legion, could be cited.

The subsection clearly evidences an intent to enforce the ordinance by seeing that individuals operate on the basis of the plans they submit and upon which permits are issued.

SECTION 8. BOARD OF ADJUSTMENT: ESTABLISHMENT AND PROCEDURE

A Board of Adjustment is hereby established, which shall consist of five members to be appointed by the City Council, each for a term of three years. Members of the Board of Adjustment may be removed from office by the City Council for cause upon written charges and after public hearing. Vacancies shall be filled by resolution of the City Council for the unexpired term of the member affected.

1. *Proceedings of the Board of Adjustment.*—The Board of Adjustment shall adopt rules necessary to the conduct of its affairs and in keeping with the provisions of this ordinance. Meetings shall be held at the call of the chairman and at such other times as the Board may determine. The chairman, or in his absence the acting chairman, may administer oaths and compel the attendance of witnesses. All meetings shall be open to the public.

The Board of Adjustment shall keep minutes of its proceedings, showing the vote of each member upon each question, or if absent or failing to vote indicating such fact, and shall keep records of its examinations and other official actions, all of which shall be a public record and be immediately filed in the office of the Board.

2. *Hearings; Appeals; Notice.*—Appeals to the Board of Adjustment concerning interpretation or administration of this ordinance may be taken by any person aggrieved or by any officer or bureau of the governing body of the city affected by any decision of the administrative official. Such appeals shall be taken within a reasonable time, not to exceed 60 days or such lesser period as may be provided by the rules of the Board, by filing with the administrative official and with the Board of Adjustment a notice of appeal specifying the grounds thereof. The administrative official shall forthwith transmit to the Board all papers constituting the record upon which the action appealed from was taken.

The Board of Adjustment shall fix a reasonable time for the hearing of appeal, give public notice thereof as well as due notice to the parties in interest, and decide the same within a reasonable time. At the hearing, any party may appear in person or by agent or attorney.

3. *Stay of Proceedings.*—An appeal stays all proceedings in furtherance of the action appealed from, unless the administrative official
from whom the appeal is taken certifies to the Board of Adjustment
after the notice of appeal is filed with him, that by reason of facts stated
in the certificate, a stay would, in his opinion, cause imminent peril to
life and property. In such case proceedings shall not be stayed other
than by a restraining order which may be granted by the Board of
Adjustment or by a court of record on application, on notice to the
administrative official from whom the appeal is taken and on due cause
shown.

COMMENTARY—SECTION 8

Since no zoning ordinance can possibly provide for all future eventualities,
some property owners will inevitably suffer hardships. Application of the
letter of the ordinance in their situations will work injustice, unless a means
is provided for granting some measure of relief. The instrument for providing
this relief and giving the requisite flexibility to a zoning ordinance is the board
of adjustment.

Some cities have called their board of adjustment a "board of appeals," a
"zoning board of appeals," a "zoning board," or other term, but the correct
nomenclature under the *Standard Act* is board of adjustment. "Adjustment"
may not be so descriptive a word as "appeals" but it is the proper one to use
if state enabling legislation is so worded. The board of adjustment serves
as a judicial or quasi-judicial agency with powers that very roughly resemble
those of a court of equity. Equity, it may be recalled, is designed to "do
justice" when justice cannot be otherwise obtained under the letter of the law.
The powers of the board of adjustment are discussed in some detail in the
commentary that follows section 9 of the model text.

Under the language of paragraph 1, section 7, of the *Standard Act*, a city
may establish a board of adjustment. Regardless of the apparently permissive
nature of the language, *no city should adopt a zoning ordinance without providing for a board of adjustment.* Having established such a board to perform
the necessary "judicial type" actions connected with zoning, the governing
body of the city should never, under any circumstances, retain for itself a
further right of appeal from the decisions of the board of adjustment (see
commentary following sections 9 and 10 of the model text).

Section 8 of the model ordinance deals with the composition and procedures
of the board of adjustment. The language of the model text parallels closely
that of the first six paragraphs of section 7 of the *Standard Act* and, for the
most part, is self-explanatory.

Under the *Standard Act*, the municipality has no alternative in establishing its board of adjustment but to provide for five members serving three-
year terms and removable for cause. Further, the members must all take

office at the same time, for the *Standard Act* is not written to provide for staggered terms. (We take the view that state enabling legislation *should* provide for staggered terms.) In some cases, cities have acted on their own initiative—and in the face of contrary provision in state enabling legislation—to provide staggering of terms for board of adjustment members. The legality of actions taken by such a board is open to doubt.

Perhaps some word needs to be said at this point about the nature of the membership of the board of adjustment. It is a well established principle of law, fortified by the American conception of "fair play," that a man should not sit in judgment in his own case or a case in which he has an interest. Unfortunately, far too many cities are utilizing their planning boards as boards of adjustment and vice versa. Planning boards are necessary mechanisms in the government of a progressive community, but their functions differ greatly from those of a board of adjustment. The members of a planning board should not, as a group, be placed in the position of serving as a board of adjustment where they may have to pass on the very recommendations that they made as a planning board. Using the same membership for both boards may be legal in the sense that it is "allowable" under the law, but such a procedure certainly violates the conceptions of simple justice and fair play.

Overlapping one, or at the most two, members of these boards has certain advantages relating to coordination and understanding, but the overlapping idea should not be extended beyond this point. It might be noted, too, that the pressure of work is often such that it is unfair to ask responsible citizens to spend time on a board that is, in effect, two boards.

A board of adjustment must, under the model text and the *Standard Act*, adopt rules to govern its proceedings, keep minutes, hold only public meetings, and maintain records of the board votes, examinations, and other official actions. All records are public records. The chairman, or vice chairman if the chairman is absent, may administer oaths and compel the attendance of witnesses.

The correct procedure in zoning administration calls for appeals from the decision of the administrative official to lie only to the board of adjustment. Such is the intent of subsection 2 of section 8 of the model text and such, we believe, is the intent of the *Standard Act*. The discretion of the administrative official is strictly limited, and he has no power to vary the letter of the ordinance and ameliorate hardships.

"Any person aggrieved" or any officer or bureau of the governing body of the city affected by the decision of the administrative official may appeal. Thus appeals may occur in a variety of circumstances: where the administrative official has refused to approve the issuance of a building permit or has refused to issue a certificate of zoning compliance; where the administrative official has approved issuance of a building permit or a certificate of zoning compliance and an affected property owner appeals; where an order, requirement, decision, or interpretation of the administrative official is called into question after an unfavorable action by the administrative official;

or where a favorable order, requirement, decision, or interpretation of the administrative official is called into question by an affected property owner.

Subsection 2 provides for adequate notice and hearing of such appeals as called for in the *Standard Act.* The language of subsection 3 is taken directly from the *Standard Act.* The effect of this slightly intricate phraseology is to stay all further activity until the decision of the board of adjustment is taken.

In emergency situations, the special procedure outlined in subsection 3 is available.

SECTION 9. THE BOARD OF ADJUSTMENT: POWERS AND DUTIES

The Board of Adjustment shall have the following powers and duties:

1. *Administrative Review.*—To hear and decide appeals where it is alleged there is error in any order, requirement, decision, or determination made by the administrative official in the enforcement of this ordinance.

2. *Special Exceptions: Conditions Governing Applications; Procedures.*—To hear and decide only such special exceptions as the Board of Adjustment is specifically authorized to pass on by the terms of this ordinance; to decide such questions as are involved in determining whether special exceptions should be granted; and to grant special exceptions with such conditions and safeguards as are appropriate under this ordinance, or to deny special exceptions when not in harmony with the purpose and intent of this ordinance. A special exception shall not be granted by the Board of Adjustment unless and until:

a) A written application for a special exception is submitted indicating the section of this ordinance under which the special exception is sought and stating the grounds on which it is requested;

b) Notice shall be given at least 15 days in advance of public hearing. The owner of the property for which special exception is sought or his agent shall be notified by mail. Notice of such hearings shall be posted on the property for which special exception is sought, at the City Hall, and in one other public place at least 15 days prior to the public hearing;

c) The public hearing shall be held. Any party may appear in person, or by agent or attorney;

d) The Board of Adjustment shall make a finding that it is empowered under the section of this ordinance described in the application to grant the special exception, and that the granting of the special exception will not adversely affect the public interest.

e) Before any special exception shall issue, the Board shall make written findings certifying compliance with the specific rules governing individual special exceptions and that satisfactory provision and arrangement has been made concerning the following, where applicable:

1) ingress and egress to property and proposed structures thereon with particular reference to automotive and pedestrian safety and convenience, traffic flow and control, and access in case of fire or catastrophe;

2) off-street parking and loading areas where required, with particular attention to the items in (1) above and the economic, noise, glare, or odor effects of the special exception on adjoining properties and properties generally in the district;

3) refuse and service areas, with particular reference to the items in (1) and (2) above;

4) utilities, with reference to locations, availability, and compatibility;

5) screening and buffering with reference to type, dimensions, and character;

6) signs, if any, and proposed exterior lighting with reference to glare, traffic safety, economic effect, and compatibility and harmony with properties in the district;

7) required yards and other open space;

8) general compatibility with adjacent properties and other property in the district.

3. *Variances; Conditions Governing Applications; Procedures.*— To authorize upon appeal in specific cases such variance from the terms of this ordinance as will not be contrary to the public interest where, owing to special conditions, a literal enforcement of the provisions of this ordinance would result in unnecessary hardship. A var-

iance from the terms of this ordinance shall not be granted by the Board of Adjustment unless and until:

a) A written application for a variance is submitted demonstrating:

   1) That special conditions and circumstances exist which are peculiar to the land, structure, or building involved and which are not applicable to other lands, structures, or buildings in the same district;

   2) That literal interpretation of the provisions of this ordinance would deprive the applicant of rights commonly enjoyed by other properties in the same district under the terms of this ordinance;

   3) That the special conditions and circumstances do not result from the actions of the applicant;

   4) That granting the variance requested will not confer on the applicant any special privilege that is denied by this ordinance to other lands, structures, or buildings in the same district.

   No non-conforming use of neighboring lands, structures, or buildings in the same district, and no permitted or non-conforming use of lands, structures, or buildings in other districts shall be considered grounds for the issuance of a variance.

b) Notice of public hearing shall be given as in Section 9 (2) (b) above;

c) The public hearing shall be held. Any party may appear in person, or by agent or by attorney;

d) The Board of Adjustment shall make findings that the requirements of Section 9 (3) (a) have been met by the applicant for a variance;

e) The Board of Adjustment shall further make a finding that the reasons set forth in the application justify the granting of the variance, and that the variance is the minimum variance that will make possible the reasonable use of the land, building, or structure;

f) The Board of Adjustment shall further make a finding that the granting of the variance will be in harmony with the general purpose and intent of this ordinance, and will not be injurious to the neighborhood, or otherwise detrimental to the public welfare.

In granting any variance, the Board of Adjustment may prescribe appropriate conditions and safeguards in conformity with this ordinance. Violation of such conditions and safeguards, when made a part of the terms under which the variance is granted, shall be deemed a violation of this ordinance and punishable under Section 16 of this ordinance.

Under no circumstances shall the Board of Adjustment grant a variance to allow a use not permissible under the terms of this ordinance in the district involved, or any use expressly or by implication prohibited by the terms of this ordinance in said district.

4. *Board Has Powers of Administrative Official on Appeals; Reversing Decision of Administrative Official.*—In exercising the above mentioned powers, the Board of Adjustment may, so long as such action is in conformity with the terms of this ordinance, reverse or affirm, wholly or partly, or may modify the order, requirement, decision, or determination appealed from and may make such order, requirement, decision, or determination as ought to be made, and to that end shall have the powers of the administrative official from whom the appeal is taken.

The concurring vote of four members of the Board shall be necessary to reverse any order, requirement, decision, or determination of the administrative official, or to decide in favor of the applicant on any matter upon which it is required to pass under this ordinance, or to effect any variation in the application of this ordinance.

COMMENTARY—SECTION 9

Previous note has been taken of the judicial or quasi-judicial nature of the powers of a board of adjustment. So far as zoning law and administration is concerned, the city governing body is the legislative, political, and policy-making authority; the administrative official is the "executive" and administrative authority; the board of adjustment is the "judicial" authority. This separation of power and function in zoning is important, just as the separation of powers principle is a vital part of American law in general.

Viewed the country over, the powers of boards of adjustment have become fairly well standardized. The national pattern closely follows the *Standard Act* in granting authority for boards of adjustment to: (1) hear and decide appeals when it is alleged that there is error in any order, decision, requirement, or determination of the administrative official; (2) to hear and decide special exceptions; and (3) to authorize, after appeal, variances from the terms of the zoning ordinance.

Section 9 of the model text is built on the base of paragraph 7, section 7, of the *Standard Act*. We have expanded this language, drawing our authority from court decisions construing the powers of boards of adjustment. The intent of section 9 is to spell out clearly the authority of a board of adjustment under the model text and to ensure that proper procedural and substantive safeguards are thrown around the authority conferred on the board.

Administrative Review. Subsection 1. Subsection 1 of section 9 of the model text deals with the first power of the board as listed above. It confers on the board of adjustment the authority to interpret the zoning ordinance when a dispute arises. The *Standard Act* and subsection 1 intend that the board of adjustment be the proper forum for making such interpretations; that the administrative official's discretion be carefully limited by the ordinance; and that the political-legislative branch of the city government not participate in making such interpretations, save only through the process of amending the ordinance.

Special Exceptions: Conditions Governing Applications; Procedures. Subsection 2. Subsection 2 deals with special exceptions. The average citizen is greatly confused over the terms "special exception" and "variance." Unfortunately this confusion extends far too frequently to members of boards of adjustment and municipal officials as well. Some boards of adjustment have used the two terms synonymously. Employment of the two terms interchangeably or as synonyms is very much in error. Even the courts sometimes exhibit a complete lack of understanding of the important differences between a special exception and a variance. Thus the Florida Supreme Court in *Troup v. Bird*, 53 So. 2d 171 (1951), not only failed completely to recognize the distinction but wrote an opinion so notable for confusion that legal commentators have cited it as an example of courts "erroneously" applying the two terms. Fortunately, *Troup v. Bird* does not represent the Florida Supreme Court's normal comprehension of zoning law and administration.

A special exception in a zoning ordinance is allowable where the facts and conditions prescribed and detailed in the ordinance as those upon which a special exception may be granted are determined by the board of adjustment to exist. In the modern zoning ordinance, provision is made in the schedule of district regulations for the precise types of uses allowed as special exceptions in each district and the requirements under which the special exceptions may be allowed. Suppose, for example, that in a particular residential district the schedule showed hospitals allowed under specified conditions as special exceptions to the use requirements applying generally to the district. Persons seeking to build a hospital in such a district would apply to the administrative official who, having no authority to grant a special exception, would deny the request. The interested parties would then go to the board of adjustment where the authority to grant the special exception, subject only to possible court review, would lie. An applicant for a special exception carries no burden of showing any unnecessary hardship; he must simply demonstrate to the board of adjustment that he meets the requirements laid down in the ordinance.

A variance, on the other hand, is granted by the board of adjustment to allow an applicant relief from the requirements of the letter of the ordinance because of unnecessary hardship or practical difficulty. For example, an individual might own a lot with a stream or pond so located on it that he simply cannot comply with the yard or setback requirements of the ordinance. A variance granted by the board of adjustment is the proper instrument to enable him to build a house on the lot.

The specific concern of the commentary at this point is with subsection 2 of section 9 of the model text and the power conferred on the board of adjustment to grant special exceptions. We frankly state that we wish to see the special exception given its correct place in the zoning law of the several states. It is a useful tool and one too long misused or not used at all.

Subsection 2 lists the procedural and substantive requirements that the applicant must meet in order to qualify for a special exception. These textual requirements apply to *all* special exceptions and are in addition to any that may appear for specific districts in the schedule of district regulations. If the schedule of district regulations does not allow an apartment house over four stories high in a specific district as a permissible use and if the schedule does not allow it as a special exception subject to prescribed conditions, then, obviously, no apartment house over four stories high can be built in that district.

Paragraph (*a*) of subsection 2 requires a written application for a special exception. In this way, all possible parties will be apprised of the precise nature of the request for a special exception and the grounds on which it is sought. Requiring a written application, too, aids a bit in cutting down frivolous and clearly unfounded requests.

Paragraph (*b*) sets out the method of giving notice that a request for a special exception is now before the board of adjustment and that action will be taken on it at a particular time. The requirements of this paragraph meet the limitations of the *Standard Act*, and even add to those limitations a bit. The hearing is a public one and any person is allowed to appear.

The board is required to find that it has the power to grant the special exception. The board is required to make a substantive finding that the grant of the special exception will not adversely affect the public interest.

Paragraph (*e*), page 52, has been added to this revision of the model text because we have found that boards of adjustment need a guide to the items that should be checked in considering applications for special exceptions. Paragraph (*e*) outlines these items clearly, and our experience has been that the boards need and appreciate this list. (Attorneys will recognize, moreover, that simply allowing a board of adjustment to grant special exceptions, without establishing standards to guide the board in the exercise of that authority, quite possibly might raise legal questions in some jurisdictions about invalid delegation of legislative power.)

The board is allowed, consistent with the ordinance, to require appropriate conditions and safeguards; the violations of these conditions and safeguards constitutes a violation of the ordinance.

We have attempted in subsection 2 to give a clear picture of procedure and substance of board authority over special exceptions. Most zoning ordinances today do not spell out the authority in this fashion. Under the model text the citizen, the various parts of the zoning machinery, and the courts should not suffer so much from doubt as to the nature, extent, and procedural requirements involved in the exercise of board power to grant special exceptions.

Variances: Conditions Governing Applications; Procedures. Subsection 3. Important as the functions of interpretation and passing on special exceptions are, some of the work of the board of adjustment under normal conditions will include passing on variances to the ordinance. It should be thoroughly understood at the outset that variances are not means for correcting bad or imperfect zoning. The city governing body, through the process of amendment, is the only proper instrument for changing an ordinance—good, bad, or indifferent. But in using its power to grant variances, the board of adjustment can usually "make or break" the entire zoning scheme. Laxness or excessive liberality can ruin the best conceived ordinance; unwarranted inflexibility in the strict application of the ordinance can induce citizen reaction against it and result in unnecessary hardship and distress.

The irreducible factor in granting a variance is "unnecessary hardship" on the applicant. The model text and the *Standard* Act so declare. Without a showing to the satisfaction of the board of adjustment that unnecessary hardship will result, the variance should not be granted. A variance issued for a lesser reason or simply because the board feels it is doing "justice" constitutes an invalid application of board authority.

But what constitutes "unnecessary hardship?" Certainly any definition depends in no small degree upon the circumstances in which its application is sought. Most zoning ordinances make no attempt at definition or delineation with the result that boards of adjustment must fend for themselves, deriving such knowledge as they may from court decisions on the topic.   The reader will note that subsection 3 of section 9 of the model text pays particular attention to factors which the board of adjustment should consider in determining whether or not granting a variance will prevent unnecessary hardship. Our intent is to outline these factors, to give boards of adjustment guides, insofar as an indefinite term can be given precise meaning. The entire subsection is grounded pretty thoroughly on judicial decisions, judge-made pronouncements of the meaning and intent of "unnecessary hardship."

Subsection 3 of section 9 of the model text sets out the framework of procedure and substantive limitation under which boards of adjustment should operate in granting variances. Because almost every requirement set out in this subsection has a basis in court decision, there is reasonable certainty that the various portions of the subsection would meet court tests, should any arise.

The board of adjustment cannot grant a variance unless and until certain things are done and certain facts are shown to be true. As in the case of special exceptions, a written application must be filed with the board of adjustment. Such an application comes to the board on appeal from the decision of the administrative official. The reasons for requiring a written application parallel those already given in setting the same requirements for special exceptions.

Paragraph (a) is an extremely important statement. Its elements constitute, for the major part, the factors that an applicant must demonstrate to bring himself within the magic formula of "unnecessary hardship." It is the intent of this paragraph that any applicant for a variance must demonstrate that *all* of the factors listed apply to his situation; the board of adjustment may not pick and choose among them.

The factors of paragraph (a) are, for the most part, self-explanatory to those having some familiarity with zoning law and administration. The applicant has no grounds for requesting a variance unless he can show that his situation is different—that literal application of the zoning ordinance will deprive him of rights commonly enjoyed by others in the same zoning district. Since a board of adjustment resembles to some degree a court of equity, the special conditions which the applicant is pleading must not be the result of his own doing. The applicant must show that granting the variance will not put him ahead of his neighbors, that is, that he will not gain any special privilege not enjoyed by the remaining lands, buildings, or structures in the district.

The final portion of paragraph (a) deserves some special comment, however, for many boards of adjustment around the nation are using the existence of non-conforming uses of neighboring lands or structures in a zoning district, or nearby uses in *other* districts, as grounds—or an excuse—for the issuance of variances. Such a utilization of non-conforming uses (and the reader is cautioned to remember how they are defined in section 4 of the model text) certainly violates principles of sound zoning administration, and in our view, is open to most serious legal questions as well. The *Standard Act* speaks only of "unnecessary hardship" as grounds for granting a variance. Presence of non-conforming uses should never be allowed as the basis for granting a variance. Nor, for that matter, should nearby uses in other zoning districts be considered in deciding whether or not a variance should issue.

For the matter of granting a variance is not, in the last analysis, based on *use*. In Florida, and in most other states as well, boards of adjustment cannot grant *use* variances at all. The Florida case of *Josephsen v. Autrey*,

96 So. 2d 784 (1957), indicates clearly that the board of adjustment cannot use its variance authority to accomplish what would, in effect, be rezoning. Numbers of cases in other jurisdictions support this view, though the use variance has been found valid in a few states. Where a board of adjustment grants use variances, as many boards in Florida and elsewhere do even though such an action is clearly invalid, it is usurping the functions of the city's governing boards, for rezoning is to be accomplished *only* through the process of formal amendment of the zoning ordinance.

We have emphasized that city governing bodies should refrain from allowing further appeals from the board of adjustment to the city council, for such a provision allows the legislative-political body to intrude on the "judicial" function of the board of adjustment. We would emphasize just as firmly that the board of adjustment should not intrude into the legislative province of the city governing body by employing a use variance to accomplish rezoning.

A variance is not a matter of *use* in the legal sense, then, save that the use must conform to the permitted uses of the district involved. Boards of adjustment are well advised to consider carefully that they have no power to grant use variances and that, therefore, they should not use neighboring non-conforming uses, nor nearby uses in other districts, to constitute a basis for judgment in granting a variance.

This entire matter is nailed down even more clearly in the last sentence of subsection 3 of section 9. "Free-wheeling" by boards of adjustment in the area of "use" is clearly prohibited. The use variance is poor zoning law and worse zoning administration. Even in those states where the use variance has been found valid, cities would be well advised, if they may legally do so, to write a prohibition against its use into the zoning ordinance.

The requirements for notice and public hearing set out in paragraphs (*b*) and (*c*) of subsection 3 parallel those for granting the handling of special exceptions outlined in subsection 2.

The findings required for granting a variance are more extensive than those necessary for a special exception. The board of adjustment must find, that is, place on the written record, that (1) the requirements of section 9 (3) (*a*) of the model text have been met; (2) that the reasons set out by the applicant justify the granting of the variance (in other words, that the applicant has demonstrated that unnecessary hardship will result to him if the variance is not granted); (3) that the variance is the minimum one that will make possible the reasonable use of the land or structure concerned; and (4) that the granting of the variance accords with the purpose and intent of the zoning ordinance and will not affect the neighborhood or general welfare adversely.

As in the case of special exceptions, the board is authorized to require appropriate conditions and safeguards, violation of which constitutes a violation of the ordinance.

Board Has Powers of Administrative Official on Appeals; Reversing De-

cision of Administrative Official. Subsection 4. This particular subsection is taken almost exactly from the *Standard Act.* The intent of the subsection is clear. Passing note may be taken of the fact, however, that some boards of adjustment occasionally act with the vote of but *three* members in the matters listed. We have even seen zoning ordinances, presumably enacted under the *Standard Act,* that specify that three members may so act! Such provisions are clearly invalid, and any action of the type listed, taken with the votes of but three members, is equally unlawful. Four votes are required; if one member of the five member board of adjustment is absent, then the four remaining members must be unanimous, if the matter is one covered by subsection 4 and the *Standard Act.*

Some General Comments on Section 9 of the Model Text. Some general comments, primarily by way of emphasis, are necessary.

While the procedures as outlined for passing on special exceptions and variances have certain similarities, the substantive showings that must be made in the two instances are quite different. Thorough understanding of the distinction by boards of adjustment is necessary.

As a matter of general procedure, the board in drawing up its own rules should probably specify that an individual denied a special exception, variance, or otherwise ruled against by the board, *on other than procedural grounds,* should not have the right to appear before the board on the *same* matter again for a specified period of time, say six months. Applicants might make a mistake in procedure, and they should not be penalized for it. But a rule of the type described will aid in protecting the board against the chronic "appealer without cause." Such a rule is lawful and desirable.

Students of administrative law will recognize that we have been careful to set standards for the guidance of the board of adjustment in the performance of its functions. Quasi-judicial or "judicial-type" power may not be granted to a body such as the board of adjustment unless that power is channeled within the limits of identifiable standards—standards that guide the agency in its activity. The board of adjustment does not operate under the model text with an absolute discretion; each act that it takes must find sanction in the ordinance and in the laws and constitution of the state.

SECTION 10. APPEALS FROM THE BOARD OF ADJUSTMENT

Any person or persons, or any board, taxpayer, department, board, or bureau of the city aggrieved by any decision of the Board of Adjustment may seek review by a court of record of such decision, in the manner provided by the laws of the State and particularly by Chapter ———, State Statutes.

COMMENTARY—SECTION 10

The courts have a role to play, and it is an important one in zoning law and administration. They represent the ultimate resort for one who feels that a decision of the board of adjustment is incorrect. The *Standard Act* recognizes the judicial function in relation to zoning by making provision for review by the courts of decisions of the board of adjustment.

Section 10 of the model text simply paraphrases the portion of section 7 of the *Standard Act* guaranteeing this right of court review. The actual procedure involved will be governed by state law; therefore, the model text makes no attempt to outline it. Those utilizing the model text should also take care that correct terminology, for the state concerned, be used in denominating the particular court which will review decisions.

Our intent is that court review of decisions of a board of adjustment be broadly afforded to interested persons, officers, or agencies. Again, however, technical questions arise as to just who "any person or persons . . . aggrieved" may be; the answer varies from state to state. The basic issue involves one known to the legal profession as "standing to sue." Readers should be aware that the language of the *Standard Act* on this point, here paraphrased, is interpreted differently in different states.

The scope of court review of a board of adjustment decision also varies from state to state. In some states, the court may review *de novo*, that is, the court may take testimony not introduced before the board of adjustment. In other states, court review is limited to the record made before the board of adjustment. In any event, boards of adjustment are always well advised to keep as complete and accurate records of their proceedings as possible against the day of possible court review.

SECTION 11. DUTIES OF ADMINISTRATIVE OFFICIAL, BOARD OF ADJUSTMENT, CITY COMMISSION, AND COURTS ON MATTERS OF APPEAL

It is the intent of this ordinance that all questions of interpretation and enforcement shall be first presented to the administrative official, and that such questions shall be presented to the Board of Adjustment only on appeal from the decision of the administrative official, and that recourse from the decisions of the Board of Adjustment shall be to the courts as provided by law and particularly by Chapter ———, State Statutes.

It is further the intent of this ordinance that the duties of the City Council in connection with this ordinance shall not include hearing and deciding questions of interpretation and enforcement that may arise. The procedure for deciding such questions shall be as stated in this section and this ordinance. Under this ordinance the City Council shall have only the duties (1) of considering and adopting or rejecting proposed amendments or the repeal of this ordinance, as provided by law, and (2) of establishing a schedule of fees and charges as stated in Section 12, below.

COMMENTARY—SECTION 11

Examination of a considerable number of zoning ordinances has led us to include a section in the model text spelling out the functions of the administrative official, board of adjustment, courts, and city governing body on matters of appeal.

Many zoning ordinances, for example, allow an appeal from the board of adjustment to the city governing body. Such a procedure, in our opinion, violates principles of sound zoning administration, injects governing body-political factors into zoning administration and may even be invalid under the *Standard Act*.

Section 11 represents an effort to demonstrate intent as to the appeal relationships of the various agencies having a part to play in the zoning law and administration. The first step is in the hands of the administrative official; the second is the responsibility of the board of adjustment; the third enters the province of the courts. The city governing body is restricted to setting fees and charges, a relatively minor function, and to the important duty of passing on amendments to the zoning ordinance.

If the provisions of this section are adhered to, the result will be orderly procedure. City governing bodies should cheer the fact that they will no longer have to serve as a second quasi-judicial appeals agency. The area of zoning law and administration that contains elements of "judicial" activity will run in the channels that it should—from the board of adjustment to the courts. From the standpoint of administrative law, the procedure is legally sound; from the standpoint of administration, the citizen will be able to ascertain precisely what the various appeals steps are.

SECTION 12. SCHEDULE OF FEES, CHARGES, AND EXPENSES

The City Council shall establish a schedule of fees, charges, and expenses and a collection procedure for building permits, certificates of zoning compliance, appeals, and other matters pertaining to this ordinance. The schedule of fees shall be posted in the office of the administrative official, and may be altered or amended only by the City Council.

Until all applicable fees, charges, and expenses have been paid in full, no action shall be taken on any application or appeal.

COMMENTARY—SECTION 12

Governmental services cost money, and the field of zoning is no exception to this rule. There are a number of areas of zoning administration, however, where valid fees can be charged, thus making the administration of the zoning ordinance partially self-supporting. So long as the size of the fee bears some reasonable relationship to the services or activity rendered, the courts hold such fee or charge systems valid.

Section 12 of the model text empowers the city's governing body to establish a system of fees and charges. Such a provision is quite common in zoning ordinances. The responsibility for setting such charges properly belongs to the governing body, though a number of cities have allowed the administrative official to establish a list of fees. The legal authority of the governing body to establish such a schedule of fees, providing they are reasonable, is unchallenged. On the other hand, unless the authorizing power is carefully drawn, legal questions can usually be raised about the power of the administrative official to draw up a schedule of fees and charges. The administrative official should not have authority to alter the schedule of fees once it has been established by the governing authority.

Notice that the section allows for charges in connection with appeals from a decision of the administrative official to the board of adjustment. These appeals do have administrative costs connected with them. The charge should not be so high as to make justice, in effect, a commodity only available to those able to afford it, but some portion at least of the minimum administrative costs connected with such an appeal should be borne by those making the appeal. To some extent, even a low fee will discourage frivolous appeals. Cities should study carefully the administrative costs involved and should set fees that reflect costs fairly accurately. In our experience, cities almost uniformly set fees that are far too low.

Section 12 of the model text requires the city's governing body to establish a collection procedure. Such a procedure is especially important in connection with the charges for appeals and similar matters. Collections for building permits, on the other hand, are relatively simple, provided the requirement that work cannot be done without a building permit is enforced!

SECTION 13. AMENDMENTS

The regulations, restrictions, and boundaries set forth in this ordinance may from time to time be amended, supplemented, changed, or repealed, provided however that no such action may be taken until after a public hearing in relation thereto, at which parties in interest and citizens shall have an opportunity to be heard. At least 15 days' notice of the time and place of such hearing shall be published in a newspaper of general circulation in the city.

When a proposed amendment affects the zoning classification of property, and in case a protest against such change is signed by the owners of 20 per cent or more either of the area of the lots included in such proposed change, or of those immediately adjacent in the rear thereof extending —— feet therefrom, or of those directly opposite thereto extending —— feet from the street frontage of such opposite lots, then such amendments shall not become effective except by the favorable vote of three-fourths of the City Council.

COMMENTARY—SECTION 13

No zoning ordinance can be drafted that will meet forever, or even for a long period of time, the requirements of a growing community. The progressive municipality will make city planning a continuous process. It will know that it cannot sit back, having once drafted a comprehensive plan and adopted a zoning ordinance, and decide that nothing further needs to be done.

Changes and amendments in the zoning ordinance will be necessary from time to time. The bulk of these changes will normally occur in the schedule of district regulation and the official zoning map. We would emphasize, however, that too great and frequent resort to the process of amendment or change, particularly when such changes are not made in conformity with an over-all community plan, will destroy the ends that planning and zoning are designed to accomplish. Changing district boundaries or regulations because of political pressure, friendship, influence, or other cause not related to the purposes of zoning results in a haphazard and ill-conceived city which is satisfactory to few citizens.

The process of amendment or change should be used cautiously and only after a full consideration of the numerous factors involved. Yet there should be a full realization, too, that change *will* be necessary. Only the completely stagnant community can afford the expensive luxury of never amending its zoning ordinance.

Section 13 of the model text outlines the process of amendment. No change can occur without public notice and hearing. The notice must be given at least 15 days in advance of the hearing and is to be published in a newspaper of general circulation in the city. The model text follows section 4 of the *Standard Act* in this regard. Note should be taken, however, that if there is no newspaper of general circulation within the municipality then the requirement of the model text must be changed to include some alternate provisions such as posting three notices of such hearing in at least three conspicuous places within the municipality, including the city or town hall. The requirement of notice of section 13 of the model text is a minimum requirement; some municipalities may wish to increase it. A city might, for example, provide for notice both in a newspaper and by public posting of the property involved.

We have not included a requirement for notice by mail to nearby property owners. Such a requirement is rather commonly found, yet no provision of the *Standard Act* makes it mandatory. (Nor is there legal bar to including the requirement, of course.) Mail notice requirements can result in large administrative headaches. Certainly if a mail notice requirment is to be included it should specify that the owners of property for this purpose shall be deemed to be those whose names appear on the latest city tax rolls, thus avoiding the problem of determining just who the owner of a property at the moment may be.

We much prefer a requirement, not included as a part of this model text, that large and conspicuous signs be posted on properties for which rezoning is sought and that full information as to the change sought and the date, time, and place of the hearing appear on the signs. Experience demonstrates that these signs constitute an alerting mechanism fully as effective and far less administratively cumbersome than the more traditional mail notice.

If a mail notice provision is to be included, however, the footage requirement (number of feet from boundaries of property for which rezoning is sought and within which property owners are to be given mail notice) should be made to square with that section of a state's enabling act dealing with the 20 per cent protest requirement.

The provision for a 20 per cent protest is taken from section 5 of the *Standard Act*, and any zoning ordinance enacted under it should include such a requirement. The language of section 13 of the model text on this point is the language of the *Standard Act*. As a matter of interpretation, the 20 per cent protest need not be from *all* of the various areas specified. Rather, a 20 per cent protest from any one is sufficient to bring into play the requirement of the *Standard Act* and the model text that a change under these circumstances cannot occur except with a three-fourths vote of the governing body of the city. Court decisions indicate pretty clearly in most states that the vote required is three-fourths of the entire governing body, not just three-fourths of a quorum. We would note that this voting requirement is being overlooked in a number of instances; such actions taken by less than three-fourths of the entire governing body, after 20 per cent protest, would be held invalid under most existing court decisions. The footage requirement varies from state to state.

As an added note on this section, some cities may wish to provide for mandatory referral of all proposed amendments to the planning board for recommendation. This is sound procedure and we have always favored it, with a proviso setting a maximum time within which the planning board must report back to the city governing body or that body may then act without the planning board's recommendation.

As a matter of procedure, most requests for the rezoning of property originate with private persons, but it is within the province of a city's governing body, its planning board, or other governmental agency to initiate such a rezoning request. A city need not wait for a private person to initiate a badly needed change.

SECTION 14. PROVISIONS OF ORDINANCE DECLARED TO BE MINIMUM REQUIREMENTS

In their interpretation and application, the provisions of this ordinance shall be held to be minimum requirements, adopted for the promotion of the public health, safety, morals, or general welfare. Wherever the requirements of this ordinance are at variance with the requirements of any other lawfully adopted rules, regulations, ordinances, deed restrictions, or covenants, the most restrictive or that imposing the higher standards, shall govern.

COMMENTARY—SECTION 14

Zoning is often only one of a number of controls at work. Deed restrictions, subdivision regulations, building codes, health regulations—all may include limitations in the form of public regulation or private contracts. Section 14 is not absolutely essential in terms of law. The courts would decide without hesitation that property prohibited from commercial use by a deed restriction could not be used for commercial purposes merely because it was located in a district in which zoning regulations permit commercial use.

Including Section 14 will, however, clarify doubts so that there is less likelihood of their being brought to the courts for resolution.

SECTION 15. COMPLAINTS REGARDING VIOLATIONS

Whenever a violation of this ordinance occurs, or is alleged to have occurred, any person may file a written complaint. Such complaint stating fully the causes and basis thereof shall be filed with the administrative official. He shall record properly such complaint, immediately investigate, and take action thereon as provided by this ordinance.

COMMENTARY—SECTION 15

Violations of zoning ordinances are uncovered in many different ways. Certainly one of the best is an active administrative machinery. Interested citizens, too, can be sources of information concerning possible deviations from the terms of the zoning ordinance.

Section 15 of the model text provides a procedure for the handling of complaints. Section 15 is designed to allow any person (and the intent is to include *any* person) to file a written complaint with the administrative official. (It will be recalled that the procedure when a violation is discovered by the administrative official is outlined in the model text, section 7, subsection 1.)

The purpose of specifying a written complaint is to cut down, so far as possible, the number of frivolous and unfounded complaints; persons who take the trouble to file a written complaint will ordinarily, though not always, have some basis for their charge. The purpose of specifying that the complaint shall be filed with the administrative official is to provide a central collecting point for such complaints and, moreover, to ensure that the administrative official has the first opportunity, as he should have under proper zoning administration, to eliminate the situation giving rise to the complaint.

The section is designed to guarantee that proper records will be kept of the complaints and that they will not be filed in the nearest wastebasket or otherwise ignored. A set of administrative rules to guide the administrative official in the procedures for recording such complaints should be set up, but such rules are not properly a part of a zoning ordinance.

SECTION 16. PENALTIES FOR VIOLATION

Violation of the provisions of this ordinance or failure to comply with any of its requirements (including violations of conditions and safeguards established in connection with grants of variances or special exceptions) shall constitute a misdemeanor. Any person who violates this ordinance or fails to comply with any of its requirements shall upon conviction thereof be fined not more than $100 or imprisoned for not more than 30 days, or both, and in addition shall pay all costs and expenses involved in the case. Each day such violation continues shall be considered a separate offense.

The owner or tenant of any building, structure, premises, or part thereof, and any architect, builder, contractor, agent, or other person who commits, participates in, assists in, or maintains such violation may each be found guilty of a separate offense and suffer the penalties herein provided.

Nothing herein contained shall prevent the city from taking such other lawful action as is necessary to prevent or remedy any violation.

COMMENTARY—SECTION 16

Under section 8 of the *Standard Act*, municipalities are empowered to provide penalties for violations of zoning ordinances. Violations of such ordinances are declared to be misdemeanors, punishable by fine or imprisonment or both.

The model zoning ordinance follows this pattern. Violation of the ordinance or failure to comply with its requirements constitute misdemeanors. The limits set, a fine of $100 or imprisonment for 30 days or both, are normally within the maximum prescribed by appropriate statutes in most states for misdemeanors. In the discretion of the judge, in the case of conviction for a violation, lesser amounts of penalty may, of course, be assessed; the amounts of penalty of section 16 are maximums.

It will be noticed that *each day* constitutes a separate offense. Such a provision is a completely legal one; it has been frequently used in other phases of law, though, ordinarily it has not been included in zoning ordinances until recently. Failure to include such language results in making enforcement of the ordinance more difficult. If the provision is not included, the result in many cases is that the chronic violator simply "buys a license" with his small fine and continues to violate the ordinance.

Thus a filling station owner, operating in violation of the ordinance, could simply pay the small one-time fine and charge it up to the "cost of doing business." In cases where the "each day a separate offense" provision would work hardship, the judiciary is the proper instrument for amelioration of of the penalty; the issue is not a proper one for zoning authorities.

The second paragraph of the section extends the application of penalties for violations to all who participate in them, making *each person* individually liable to these penalties. This sort of provision is now fairly standard in zoning ordinances.

Under the *Standard Act* the city is empowered to provide civil penalties for violation of a zoning ordinance. While the model ordinance makes no direct mention of civil process, the city may take lawful civil action under many other pertinent state statutes to ensure compliance. Thus no direct reference to civil process is usually necessary. The last sentence of section 16 is added simply to ensure that the courts will not limit the city solely to the criminal penalties expressed in the first parts of section 16.

SECTION 17. SEPARABILITY CLAUSE

Should any section or provision of this ordinance be declared by the courts to be unconstitutional or invalid, such decision shall not affect the validity of the ordinance as a whole, or any part thereof other than the part so declared to be unconstitutional or invalid.

COMMENTARY—SECTION 17

All modern legislation customarily contains what is know as a "separability" clause. The intent of this clause is to ensure that should one section of the ordinance or statute be found unconstitutional or invalid, the remaining sections will continue in force.

Actually, the separability clause gives most drafters a false sense of security. Notwithstanding the inclusion of such a clause, the courts may find a single section invalid and then find that the section is so basic to the operation of the ordinance that the ordinance as a whole must be declared invalid. If by some stretch of the imagination, for example, a court were to find the schedule of district regulations of a zoning ordinance invalid, the entire ordinance would certainly be declared invalid, and properly so. Since the schedule of district regulations is the heart of the ordinance, the remaining sections would be useless without it.

Nevertheless, incorporation of a separability clause is necessary and we have followed this usual practice in the model text.

SECTION 18. DEFINITIONS

For the purposes of this ordinance, certain terms or words used herein shall be interpreted as follows:

The word *person* includes a firm, association, organization, partnership, trust, company, or corporation as well as an individual.

The present tense includes the future tense, the singular number includes the plural, and the plural number includes the singular.

The word *shall* is mandatory, the word *may* is permissive.

The words *used* or *occupied* include the words *intended, designed, or arranged to be used or occupied.*

The word *lot* includes the words *plot* or *parcel.*

Accessory Use or Structure.—A use or structure on the same lot with, and of a nature customarily incidental and subordinate to, the principal use or structure.

Buildable Area.—The portion of a lot remaining after required yards have been provided.

Drive-In Restaurant or Refreshment Stand.—Any place or premises used for sale, dispensing, or serving of food, refreshments, or beverages in automobiles, including those establishments where customers may serve themselves and may eat or drink the food, refreshments, or beverages on the premises.

Dwelling, Single-Family.—A detached residential dwelling unit other than a mobile home, designed for and occupied by one family only.

Dwelling, Mobile Home.—A detached residential dwelling unit designed for transportation after fabrication on streets or highways on its own wheels or on flatbed or other trailers, and arriving at the site where it is to be occupied as a dwelling complete and ready for occupancy except for minor and incidental unpacking and assembly operations, location on jacks or other temporary or permanent foundations, connections to utilities, and the like. A travel trailer is not to be considered as a mobile home.

Dwelling, Two-Family.—A detached residential building containing two dwelling units, designed for occupancy by not more than two families.

Dwelling, Multiple-Family.—A residential building designed for or occupied by three or more families, with the number of families in residence not exceeding the number of dwelling units provided.

Dwelling Unit.—One room, or rooms connected together, constituting a separate, independent housekeeping establishment for owner occupancy, or rental or lease on a weekly, monthly, or longer basis, and physically separated from any other rooms or dwelling units which may be in the same structure, and containing independent cooking and sleeping facilities.

Family.—One or more persons occupying a single dwelling unit, provided that unless all members are related by blood or marriage, no such family shall contain over five persons, but further provided that domestic servants employed on the premises may be housed on the premises without being counted as a family or families.

Filling Station.—Buildings and premises where gasoline, oil, grease, batteries, tires, and automobile accessories may be supplied and dispensed at retail, and where in addition the following services may be rendered and sales made, and no other:

- *a*) Sale and servicing of spark plugs, batteries, and distributors and distributor parts;

- *b*) Tire servicing and repair, but not recapping or regrooving;

- *c*) Replacement of mufflers and tail pipes, water hose, fan belts, brake fluid, light bulbs, fuses, floor mats, seat covers, windshield wipers and wiper blades, grease retainers, wheel bearings, mirrors, and the like;

- *d*) Radiator cleaning and flushing;

- *e*) Washing and polishing, and sale of automotive washing and polishing materials;

- *f*) Greasing and lubrication;

- *g*) Providing and repairing fuel pumps, oil pumps, and lines;

- *h*) Minor servicing and repair of carburetors;

- *i*) Emergency wiring repairs;

- *j*) Adjusting and repairing brakes;

- *k*) Minor motor adjustments not involving removal of the head or crankcase or racing the motor;

- *l*) Sales of cold drinks, packaged foods, tobacco, and similar convenience goods for filling stations customers, as accessory and incidental to principal operation;

m) Provision of road maps and other informational material to customers; provision of restroom facilities.

Uses permissible at a filling station do not include major mechanical and body work, straightening of body parts, painting, welding, storage of automobiles not in operating condition, or other work involving noise, glare, fumes, smoke, or other characteristics to an extent greater than normally found in filling stations. A filling station is not a repair garage nor a body shop.

Home Occupation.—An occupation conducted in a dwelling unit, provided that:

a) No person other than members of the family residing on the premises shall be engaged in such occupation;

b) The use of the dwelling unit for the home occupation shall be clearly incidental and subordinate to its use for residential purposes by its occupants, and not more than 25 per cent of the floor area of the dwelling unit shall be used in the conduct of the home occupation;

c) There shall be no change in the outside appearance of the building or premises, or other visible evidence of the conduct of such home occupation other than one sign, not exceeding one square-foot in area, non-illuminated, and mounted flat against the wall of the principal building;

d) No home occupation shall be conducted in any accessory building;

e) There shall be no sales in connection with such home occupation;

f) No traffic shall be generated by such home occupation in greater volumes than would normally be expected in a residential neighborhood, and any need for parking generated by the conduct of such home occupation shall be met off the street and other than in a required front yard.

g) No equipment or process shall be used in such home occupation which creates noise, vibration, glare, fumes, odors, or electrical interference detectable to the normal senses off the lot, if the occupation is conducted in a single-family residence, or outside the dwelling unit if conducted in other than a single-family residence. In the case of electrical interference, no equipment or process shall be used which creates visual or audible interference in any radio or television receivers off the premises, or causes fluctuations in line voltage off the premises.

Loading Space, Off-Street.—Space logically and conveniently located for bulk pickups and deliveries, scaled to delivery vehicles expected to be used, and accessible to such vehicles when required off-street parking spaces are filled. Required off-street loading space is not to be included as off-street parking space in computation of required off-street parking space.

Lot.—For purposes of this ordinance, a lot is a parcel of land of at least sufficient size to meet minimum zoning requirements for use, coverage, and area, and to provide such yards and other open spaces as are herein required. Such lot shall have frontage on an improved public street, or on an approved private street, and may consist of:

a) A single lot of record;

b) A portion of a lot of record;

c) A combination of complete lots of record, of complete lots of record and portions of lots of record, or of portions of lots of record;

d) A parcel of land described by metes and bounds;

provided that in no case of division or combination shall any residual lot or parcel be created which does not meet the requirements of this ordinance.

Lot Frontage.—The front of a lot shall be construed to be the portion nearest the street. For the purposes of determining yard requirements on corner lots and through lots, all sides of a lot adjacent to streets shall be considered frontage, and yards shall be provided as indicated under *Yards* in this section.

Lot Measurements.—

a) *Depth* of a lot shall be considered to be the distance between the midpoints of straight lines connecting the foremost points of the side lot lines in front and the rearmost points of the side lot lines in the rear.

b) *Width* of a lot shall be considered to be the distance between straight lines connecting front and rear lot lines at each side of the lot, measured across the rear of the required front yard, provided however that width between side lot lines at their foremost points (where they intersect with the street line) shall not be less than 80 per cent of the required lot width except in the case of lots on the turning circle of culs-de-sac, where the 80 per cent requirement shall not apply.

Lot of Record.—A lot which is part of a subdivision recorded in the office of the [County Clerk, County Recorder], or a lot or parcel described by metes and bounds, the description of which has been so recorded.

Lot Types.—The diagram (Figure 1) which follows illustrates terminology used in this ordinance with reference to *corner* lots, *interior* lots, *reversed frontage* lots and *through* lots:

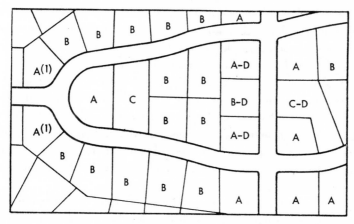

FIGURE 1

In the diagram, A=*corner* lot, defined as a lot located at the intersection of two or more streets. A lot abutting on a curved street or streets shall be considered a corner lot if straight lines drawn from the foremost points of the side lot lines to the foremost point of the lot meet at an interior angle of less than 135 degrees. See lots marked A[(1)] in the diagram.

B=*interior* lot, defined as a lot other than a corner lot with only one frontage on a street.

C=*through* lot, defined as a lot other than a corner lot with frontage on more than one street. Through lots abutting two streets may be referred to as double frontage lots.

D=*reversed frontage* lot, defined as a lot on which the frontage is at right angles or approximately right angles (interior angle less than 135 degrees) to the general pattern in the area. A reversed frontage lot may also be a corner lot (A-D in the diagram), an interior lot (B-D) or a through lot (C-D).

Outdoor Advertising Business.—Provision of outdoor displays or display space on a lease or rental basis only.

Parking Space, Off-Street.—For the purposes of this ordinance, an off-street parking space shall consist of a space adequate for parking an automobile with room for opening doors on both sides, together with properly related access to a public street or alley and maneuvering room. Required off-street parking areas for three or more automobiles shall have individual spaces marked, and shall be so designed, maintained, and regulated that no parking or maneuvering incidental to parking shall be on any public street, walk, or alley, and so that any automobile may be parked and unparked without moving another.

For purposes of rough computation, an off-street parking space and necessary access and maneuvering room may be estimated at 300 square feet, but off-street parking requirements will be considered to be met only when actual spaces meeting the requirements above are provided and maintained, improved in a manner appropriate to the circumstances of the case, and in accordance with all ordinances and regulations of the city.

Sign.—Any device designed to inform or attract the attention of persons not on the premises on which the sign is located, provided however that the following shall not be included in the application of the regulations herein:

a) Signs not exceeding one square foot in area and bearing only property numbers, post box numbers, names of occupants of premises, or other identification of premises not having commercial connotations;

b) Flags and insignia of any government except when displayed in connection with commercial promotion;

c) Legal notices; identification, informational, or directional signs erected or required by governmental bodies;

d) Integral decorative or architectural features of buildings, except letters, trademarks, moving parts, or moving lights;

e) Signs directing and guiding traffic and parking on private property, but bearing no advertising matter.

Signs, Number and Surface Area.—For the purpose of determining number of signs, a sign shall be considered to be a single display surface or display device containing elements organized, related, and composed to form a unit. Where matter is displayed in a random manner without organized relationship of elements, or where there is reasonable doubt about the relationship of elements, each element shall be considered to be a single sign.

The surface area of a sign shall be computed as including the entire area within a regular geometric form or combinations of regular geometric forms comprising all of the display area of the sign and including all of the elements of the matter displayed. Frames and structural members not bearing advertising matter shall not be included in computation of surface area.

Sign, On-Site.—A sign relating in its subject matter to the premises on which it is located, or to products, accommodations, services, or activities on the premises. On-site signs do not include signs erected by the outdoor advertising industry in the conduct of the outdoor advertising business.

Sign, Off-Site.—A sign other than an on-site sign.

Special Exception.—A special exception is a use that would not be appropriate generally or without restriction throughout the zoning division or district but which, if controlled as to number, area, location, or relation to the neighborhood, would promote the public health, safety, welfare, morals, order, comfort, convenience, appearance, prosperity, or general welfare. Such uses may be permitted in such zoning division or district as special exceptions, if specific provision for such special exceptions is made in this zoning ordinance.

Street Line.—The right-of-way line of a street.

Structure.—Anything constructed or erected with a fixed location on the ground, or attached to something having a fixed location on the ground. Among other things, structures include buildings, mobile homes, walls, fences, billboards, and poster panels.

Travel Trailer.—A vehicular, portable structure built on a chassis, designed to be used as a temporary dwelling for travel and recreational purposes, having a body width not exceeding eight feet.

Variance.—A variance is a relaxation of the terms of the zoning ordinance where such variance will not be contrary to the public interest and where, owing to conditions peculiar to the property and not the result of the actions of the applicant, a literal enforcement of the ordinance would result in unnecessary and undue hardship. As used in this ordinance, a variance is authorized only for height, area, and size of structure or size of yards and open spaces; establishment or expansion of a use otherwise prohibited shall not be allowed by variance, nor shall a variance be granted because of the presence of non-conformities in the zoning district or uses in an adjoining zoning district.

Yard.—A required open space other than a court unoccupied and unobstructed by any structure or portion of a structure from 30 inches above the general ground level of the graded lot upward, provided however that fences, walls, poles, posts, and other customary yard accessories, ornaments, and furniture may be permitted in any yard subject to height limitations and requirements limiting obstruction of visibility.

Yard, Front.—A yard extending between side lot lines across the front of a lot adjoining a public street.

In any required front yard, no fence or wall shall be permitted which materially impedes vision across such yard above the height of 30 inches, and no hedge or other vegetation shall be permitted which materially impedes vision across such yard between the heights of 30 inches and 10 feet.

In the case of through lots, unless the prevailing front yard pattern on adjoining lots indicates otherwise, front yards shall be provided on all frontages. Where one of the front yards that would normally be required on a through lot is not in keeping with the prevailing yard pattern, the administrative official may waive the requirement for the normal front yard and substitute therefor a special yard requirement which shall not exceed the average of the yards provided on adjacent lots.

In the case of corner lots which do not have reversed frontage, a front yard of the required depth shall be provided in accordance with the prevailing yard pattern and a second front yard of half the depth required generally for front yards in the district shall be provided on the other frontage.

In the case of reversed frontage corner lots, a front yard of the required depth shall be provided on either frontage, and a second front yard of half the depth required generally for front yards in the district shall be provided on the other frontage.

In the case of corner lots with more than two frontages, the administrative official shall determine the front yard requirements, subject to the following limitations: (1) At least one front yard shall be provided having the full depth required generally in the district; (2) No other front yard on such lot shall have less than half the full depth required generally.

Depth of required front yards shall be measured at right angles to a straight line joining the foremost points of the side lot lines. The foremost point of the side lot line, in the case of rounded property corners at street intersections, shall be assumed to be the point at which the side and front lot lines would have met without such rounding. Front and rear front yard lines shall be parallel.

Yard, Side.—A yard extending from the rear line of the required front yard to the rear lot line, or in the absence of any clearly defined rear lot line to the point on the lot farthest from the intersection of the lot line involved with the public street. In the case of *through lots*, side yards shall extend from the rear lines of front yards required. In the case of *corner lots*, yards remaining after full- and half-depth front yards have been established shall be considered side yards.

Width of a required side yard shall be measured in such a manner that the yard established is a strip of the minimum width required by district regulations with its inner edge parallel with the side lot line.

Yard, Rear.—A yard extending across the rear of the lot between inner side yard lines. In the case of through lots and corner lots, there will be no rear yards, but only front and side yards.

Depth of a required rear yard shall be measured in such a manner that the yard established is a strip of the minimum width required by district regulations with its inner edge parallel with the rear lot line.

Yard, Special.—A yard behind any required yard adjacent to a public street, required to perform the same functions as a side or rear yard, but adjacent to a lot line so placed or oriented that neither the term "side yard" nor the term "rear yard" clearly applies. In such cases, the administrative official shall require a yard with minimum dimensions as generally required for a side yard or a rear yard in the district, determining which shall apply by the relation of the portion of the lot on which the yard is to be located to the adjoining lot or lots, with due regard to the orientation and location of structures and buildable areas thereon.

The diagram (Figure 2) on the next page illustrates location and methods of measuring yards on rectangular and non-rectangular lots.

COMMENTARY—SECTION 18

We have no wish to join the argument that rages among legislative drafters as to the proper location of the definitions section of an ordinance or bill. Most drafters resolve the problem by placing the definitions section at the beginning, arguing that such placement gives the reader basic understandings he will need to understand the remainder of the ordinance. Those who have watched an attorney reading such an ordinance will know, however, that he is constantly flipping the pages back to the definitions section. It would appear that it makes very little difference where the definitions section is placed.

Familiarity with numerous zoning ordinances has led us to conclude that (1) far too many words are defined, (2) there is scarcely a zoning ordinance in existence today that does not define words that are not used in the ordinance at all, and (3) there is scarcely a definitions section in an ordinance today that does not omit basic words that do need definition. We are convinced that these three deficiencies arise from many causes, but one may be that the definitions section in most instances is written before the rest of the ordinance is drafted. Definitions are copied because they *might* be used, and no final check is taken to ensure the definitions of words not used are eliminated and that all words needing explanation have been defined. We have placed the definitions section of the model text at the end of the ordinance for purely psychological reasons. It is best to draft this section last. Its placement has no legal significance.

By placing the definitions section at the end of the ordinance, perhaps drafters of future zoning ordinances will tend to make the necessary checks before attempting to draft the section.

Drafters of zoning ordinances, or any other legislation for that matter, should always ask themselves, when listing words that appear to need definition, "Why do we need to define these particular words?" The answer is obvious but usually overlooked. Certain words and terms are defined in order to simplify, clarify, and make the ordinance more understandable. All other reasons for defining words or terms can be simplified in the end to this one.

Definitions are as much a part of the final ordinance as any other section. Because the principles of statutory construction *do* recognize that the pur-

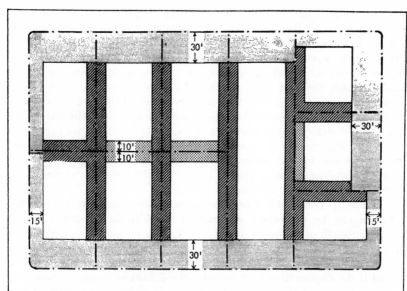

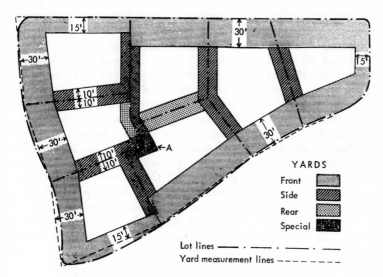

YARDS

Front
Side
Rear
Special

Lot lines ———— · ———— · ———— · ————
Yard measurement lines — — — — — — —

The illustration here assumes front yard depths required at 30 ft.
(half-depth front yards 15') side yard widths 10 ft., and rear
yard depths 10 ft. Note that at A, a special yard is shown,
indicating treatment where usual side or rear yard terminology
would be difficult to apply but purpose of the yard is clear.

LOCATION AND MEASUREMENT OF YARDS ON LOTS
FIGURE 2

pose is to clarify and simplify, the definitions section should be one of the strongest parts of the ordinance. Unfortunately far too many definitions sections in zoning ordinances are simply copied from other ordinances. Those drafters who copy will often fail to take into consideration important local factors—economic, social, geographic, or demographic. Some ordinances drafted within the past year, for example, have contained definitions of such terms as "livery stable," though livery stables have long since passed from the American scene. Perhaps there may be need for definition of certain types of stables, but if there is a livery stable anywhere, we have yet to discover it. It is difficult to believe the ordinances containing this definition—and we can cite tens of others equally absurd—were checked before enactment. A definitions section cannot be one of the strongest sections in a zoning ordinance if this approach is taken.

A carefully drawn definitions section will often mean that threatened litigation can be settled out of court. A considerable number of zoning disputes, though of course by no means all, turn on questions of definition. It would be difficult to calculate the amount of money that a city can save in litigation by taking extreme care with the definitions section.

And if the dispute should get to court, the definitions section is even more important. Courts look to definition sections in order to determine the intent of the drafters in using particular words. Great weight is normally given to these definitions. This does not mean that the judges ignore the other sections of the ordinance in determining intent, but the definitions section is one of the major highway signs on the road to decision. If the sign is unclear, the judges can lose their way just as motorists sometimes find themselves lost because of poorly marked detours.

What words used in a zoning ordinance (remember that the schedule of district regulations is a part of the ordinance) should be chosen for definition? Are there any criteria that will aid in the selection?

As a first and obvious principle, words not used anywhere in the ordinance should not be defined. A careful check of the ordinance including the schedule of district regulations will prevent this all too common transgression.

A second principle might be stated by today's slang-happy teenager quite simply as "Don't get definition-happy." Definitions sections of most zoning ordinances are filled with words that simply do not need defining. The words may have commonly and universally accepted dictionary meanings, or perhaps the courts have given such clear meaning to them that to define such terms is a waste of paper, time, and ink.

There is another category of words that does not need definition, however. These are words that are, in effect, defined at the point they are used in the ordinance. The definitions section of the model text, for example, contains no definition of "non-conforming use." To many students of zoning law and administration failure to include this basic term in the definition sections will amount to rank heresy. The reader will recall, however, that the various types of non-conformities are thoroughly and necessarily defined in section 4 of the model text—the definition was an essential part of the text.

There is a third principle that approaches the problem from the positive side: define a word or term which is used to simplify and cut down on verbiage in the ordinance. Rather than repeat throughout the ordinance "The Board of Adjustment of the City of Gainesville, Florida," reduce the phrase to "the board of adjustment" or, perhaps, "board" and then define it. Similar examples will come to mind. This idea is useful primarily where lengthy phrases, used *frequently* throughout the ordinance, may be reduced to a single word or short phrase.

As a fourth principle, remember that a technical term will need definition, unless there is a universally accepted judicial construction of such a term. The model text in section 18 defines "Accessory use or structure." This is a term that probably would be found in a schedule of district regulations; hence, we have defined it. The term is a technical one. There is some argument about its precise meaning in zoning law, though there is general agreement about its broader context.

Definitions may also serve to clear up ambiguities—or to create them. Anyone who has watched the average citizen trying to make sense out of the written definitions of the various types of yards or lot measurements can appreciate this principle. A diagram sometimes is very useful. Diagrams are valid legal instruments for defining, and cities will be well advised to utilize them as part of the definitions section of the ordinance. We have included two diagrams as a part of section 18 of the model text—and might well have included more.

In drafting section 18 of the model ordinance we have attempted to follow our own preaching, but there is no doubt that the job of defining only those words that need definition is a difficult one. So far as the text of a model ordinance is concerned, the task becomes doubly difficult, for we do not have before us the schedule of district regulations, which must be drafted at the local level if it is to have real meaning.

The result, in section 18, is a compromise. Textual terms that we believe require definition have been defined. There are not many of these, for some are defined in the text at the point where they are used and others have generally accepted meanings.

We also have tried to do some selective guessing as to terms that most cities would use in their schedules of district regulations. "Multiple-family dwelling" and "single-family dwelling" are examples of this type.

We have taken some terms long used in a traditional context and given them different or revised meanings, and we have defined some terms not ordinarily included. Sign control, for example, was not much of an issue 20 years ago. Cities today are feeling their way in this important area of regulation.

Space limitations make it impossible to list all the terms which might be defined in connection with a specific local situation.

We trust that most of the definitions are clear. A few do require specific comment.

Drive-In Restaurant or Refreshment Stand. Self-service hamburger and drink stands have been appearing in great numbers since World War II; the older concept of a "drive-in" utilizing female "car hops" has well nigh disappeared. In several court cases, judges have held that a self-service operation is *not* a "drive-in" restaurant. These self-service operations have thus been erected in zoning districts where regular restaurants could be erected but the traditional "drive-in" could not. It is necessary to so define the "drive-in" restaurant as to make it absolutely certain that self-service activities will go only in zones where the traditional drive-in would be permitted.

Dwellings—Various. Carefully drafted definitions of the various types of dwellings and of what constitutes a dwelling unit are essential. Local policy may require that the definition of "dwelling unit" be varied; the definition given might not be satisfactory, for example, in resort areas.

Because of the increasing importance in many, if not in most, parts of the country, a definition of "mobile home" has been included. The mobile home has been distinguished from the "travel trailer"; the distinction is one that must be drawn if regulation of mobile homes and travel trailers is to be meaningful.[12]

Family. If the drafters of a zoning ordinance mean to enforce the requirements on single-family, two-family, and multiple-family dwellings, there must be some definition of what constitutes the "family." The definition is definitely intended to prevent fraternity and sorority houses, or even a boarding house that might be organized under nonprofit status, from taking on a single-family status. There have been a number of court cases on this point, and it appears wise to include a definition of the type given.

Filling Station. The ubiquitous automobile service station, or filling station, is a permanent part of the American landscape. Many times, however, it becomes a great deal more than a service station. Some degenerate into full-scale repair garages or become centers for trailer and truck rentals. We apologize for the length of the definition, but we have found it very useful in making sure that a filling station stays a filling station—no more and no less. If the drafters of a zoning ordinance want to permit trailer and truck rentals, a provision to that effect can be added.

Home Occupation. In earlier editions of the model text, we rejected the inclusion of a definition of "home occupation." The omission was a mistake, and we were so informed in no uncertain terms. Drafters using the model

---

[12] City officials having special problems in dealing with mobile homes or desiring background information are referred to BAIR, LOCAL REGULATION OF MOBILE HOME PARKS, TRAVEL TRAILER PARKS, AND RELATED FACILITIES (Mobile Home Research Foundation, 20 North Wacker Drive, Chicago, Illinois, 1965), or to BARTLEY and BAIR, MOBILE HOME PARKS AND COMPREHENSIVE COMMUNITY PLANNING (University of Florida Public Administration Clearing Service, Gainesville, Florida, 1960).

text can easily expand or contract the breadth of the definition given and adapt it to particular circumstances. An author using his home for the writing of books can occasion no difficulty of any kind for his neighbors (unless he uses his neighbors as the basis for the characters in his novels!). On the other hand, a welding shop in a carport is scarcely a use that is compatible with most residential neighborhoods.

The regulation of home occupations is a delicate matter and highly controversial. Local policy can subject the term to great variation in meaning. The definition used in the model text should be most carefully examined before applying it without change to any specific community. We want to note, further, that any zoning provisions on home occupations should be carefully tracked to local ordinances on occupational license taxes. If a businessman must pay an occupational license tax, it would appear logical that a home occupation should also be subject to such a tax, though not, most probably, in the same amount.

Loading Space, Off-Street. Every ordinance should require off-street loading space for business and industrial use. We have chosen a flexible definition for this term. In some instances, ordinances are written with specific space requirements, *e.g.*, "12 feet wide by 45 feet long with 12 foot vertical clearance" and appropriate provision for ingress and egress. The disadvantage of such specific requirements is that many business activities do require off-street loading space but do not use vehicles of this size. Experience has shown the definition given to be satisfactory.

Lot. A definition of this term is necessary because we have used it in a special and specific sense as applied to zoning. The definition as given is fairly new and is not found in most zoning ordinances today. The word "lot" may be used in a variety of ways, and it is unwise in a zoning ordinance to ignore this fact. The reader will want to take the definition of *lot* and check it back against sections of the model text, for example, section 4, subsection 2.

Lot Frontage. Strangely enough, inclusion of a definition of lot frontage is a relatively new idea. Yet determination of what constitutes frontage can be extremely important. The definition should be read in conjunction with the pertinent materials under *yards*.

Lot Types. Most of the material included here is traditional. One might even argue that there is no need to include the bulk of it, since the matters defined are very nearly in the "generally accepted" category. The only item of real importance is the 135 degree criterion. Inclusion of this verbiage is necessary because of the increasing resort to curvilinear layout in many subdivisions.

Outdoor Advertising Business. Very few zoning ordinances recognize that the outdoor advertising business is a legitimate business which should be distinguished from the process of sign erection as such. Our definition gives the business the status it deserves.

Parking Space, Off-Street. Fortunately, requirements for off-street parking are now becoming common in zoning ordinances. The courts have usually sanctioned such requirements, though drafters should check the law of their state on the point. More and more citizens are beginning to recognize that streets are for traffic movement, not for parking at the expense of the tax-payer. Space for maneuvering necessary to parking should not intrude on public ways. The definition given is designed to give flexibility while ensuring adequate basis for establishing off-street parking requirements. The number of off-street parking spaces required for specific uses would appear, of course, in the schedule of district regulations.

Sign. The emphasis on signs in the definitions section is proper, for cities are now realizing that sign and billboard control is necessary in this age of advertising. Many cities, however, are uncertain as to how to proceed. In studying the various definitions dealing with signs, it should be recalled that the word "structure" is defined broadly enough to include signs. The approach taken by us to a definition of *sign* is based on a technique of exclusion. Cities should welcome this approach, providing it is the intent of the city to see that signs are regulated.

Signs, Number and Surface Area. Inclusion of this definition makes clear how the number of signs to be allowed shall be determined. This material is not found in most present day zoning ordinances. Surface area determination provisions are more common.

Sign, On-Site and Off-Site. Customarily these definitions, important as they are, have not been included in zoning ordinances.

Yard. This definition has a twist in it not commonly found. The 30 inch feature contrasts strongly with the conventional "from the ground upward" approach. The definition in the model text is intended to permit drives, walks, low terraces, swimming pools, etc. in yards. The "ground upwards" language necessitates having to torture the schedule of district regulations with all sorts of exceptions in order to include these adjuncts of modern living.

Yard, Front. Provisions for front yards on all frontages, with the exceptions noted, is a bit of an innovation. The role played by the administrative official is determined with considerable precision so that his discretion is carefully limited.

Yard, Side, and Yard, Rear. The definitions given represent a departure from accepted definitions. Yet the departure is so logical that many will wonder why it was not taken long ago.

The traditional definition runs the side yard from the rear of the front yard to the front of the rear yard; this makes necessary the provisions of special set-back requirements from the side lot lines in rear yards. The old rear yard definition, while permitting accessory structures in rear yards, specified that no part of the principal building could extend into the rear yard. These requirements probably arose from the necessity of keeping stables away from the main structure.

Now that the stable is no longer a part of American life, there seems to be no reason for keeping all parts of the principal building out of the traditional rear yard area. The approach taken in the definitions provides much greater flexibility in the use of buildable area. The rear yard becomes a true yard, but shallower than the conventional rear yard. Architects have approved this new concept. Requirements as to percentage of ground area that may be used for the principal building still act to prevent overbuilding of the lot. "L-shaped" houses, with their patios and swimming pool potentials, now become practical on smaller lots.

SECTION 19. REPEAL OF CONFLICTING ORDINANCES; EFFECTIVE DATE

All ordinances or parts of ordinances in conflict with this zoning ordinance, or inconsistent with the provisions of this ordinance, are hereby repealed to the extent necessary to give this ordinance full force and effect. This ordinance shall become effective on [date].

COMMENTARY—SECTION 19

The form for this section will vary considerably according to usage in various states. Both repeal of conflicting ordinances and effective date must be covered. Where possible, it is best to specify by number, title, or otherwise the ordinances or portions of ordinances being repealed. Where a new zoning ordinance is being enacted to replace an old one, this is no difficult matter. The relationship of zoning to other tools of planning is such that "catch-all" language of the type used above may result unwittingly in the repeal of material in other ordinances that should be retained.

APPENDICES

APPENDIX A

A Standard State Zoning Enabling Act*

SECTION 1. GRANT OF POWER.—For the purpose of promoting health, safety, morals, or the general welfare of the community, the legislative body of cities and incorporated villages is hereby empowered to regulate and restrict the height, number of stories, and size of buildings and other structures, the percentage of lot that may be occupied, the size of yards, courts, and other open spaces, the density of population, and the location and use of buildings, structures, and land for trade, industry, residence, or other purposes.

SECTION 2. DISTRICTS.—For any or all of said purposes the local legislative body may divide the municipality into districts of such number, shape, and area as may be deemed best suited to carry out the purposes of this act; and within such districts it may regulate and restrict the erection, construction, reconstruction, alteration, repair, or use of buildings, structures, or land. All such regulations shall be uniform for each class or kind of buildings throughout each district, but the regulations in one district may differ from those in other districts.

SECTION 3. PURPOSES IN VIEW.—Such regulations shall be made in accordance with a comprehensive plan and designed to lessen congestion in the streets; to secure safety from fire, panic, and other dangers; to promote health and the general welfare; to provide adequate light and air; to prevent the overcrowding of land; to avoid undue concentration of population; to facilitate the adequate provision of transportation, water, sewerage, schools, parks, and other public requirements. Such regulations shall be made with reasonable consideration, among other things, given to the character of the district and its peculiar suitability for particular uses, and with a view to conserving the value of buildings and encouraging the most appropriate use of land throughout such municipality.

SECTION 4. METHOD OF PROCEDURE.—The legislative body of such municipality shall provide for the manner in which such regulations and restrictions and the boundaries of such districts shall be determined, established, and enforced, and from time to time amended, supplemented, or changed. However, no such regulation, restriction, or boundary shall become effective until after a public hearing in relation thereto, at which parties in interest and citizens shall have an opportunity to be heard. At least 15 days' notice of the time and place of such hearing shall be published in an official paper, or a paper of general circulation, in such municipality.

SECTION 5. CHANGES.—Such regulations, restrictions, and boundaries may from time to time be amended, supplemented, changed, modified, or repealed. In case, however, of a protest against such changes, signed by the owners

* Advisory Committee on Zoning, Department of Commerce, A STANDARD STATE ZONING ENABLING ACT UNDER WHICH MUNICIPALITIES MAY ADOPT ZONING REGULATIONS (rev. ed., 1926).

of 20 per cent or more either of the area of the lots included in such proposed change, or of those immediately adjacent in the rear thereof extending ———— feet therefrom, or of those directly opposite thereto extending ———— feet from the street frontage of such opposite lots, such amendment shall not become effective except by the favorable vote of three-fourths of all the members of the legislative body of such municipality. The provisions of the previous section relative to public hearing and official notice shall apply equally to all changes or amendments.

SECTION 6. ZONING COMMISSION.—In order to avail itself of the powers conferred by this act, such legislative body shall appoint a commission, to be known as the zoning commission, to recommend the boundaries of the various original districts and appropriate regulations to be enforced therein. Such commission shall make a preliminary report and hold public hearings thereon before submitting its final report, and such legislative body shall not hold its public hearings or take action until it has received the final report of such commission. Where a city plan commission already exists, it may be appointed as the zoning commission.

SECTION 7. BOARD OF ADJUSTMENT.—Such local legislative body may provide for the appointment of a board of adjustment, and in the regulations and restrictions adopted pursuant to the authority of this act may provide that the said board of adjustment may, in appropriate cases and subject to appropriate conditions and safeguards, make special exceptions to the terms of the ordinance in harmony with its general purpose and intent and in accordance with general or specific rules therein contained.

The board of adjustment shall consist of five members, each to be appointed for a term of three years and removable for cause by the appointing authority upon written charges and after public hearing. Vacancies shall be filled for the unexpired term of any member whose term becomes vacant.

The board shall adopt rules in accordance with the provisions of any ordinance adopted pursuant to this act. Meetings of the board shall be held at the call of the chairman and at such other times as the board may determine. Such chairman, or in his absence the acting chairman, may administer oaths and compel the attendance of witnesses. All meetings of the board shall be open to the public. The board shall keep minutes of its proceedings, showing the vote of each member upon each question, or, if absent or failing to vote, indicating such fact, and shall keep records of its examinations and other official actions, all of which shall be immediately filed in the office of the board and shall be a public record.

Appeals to the board of adjustment may be taken by any person aggrieved or by any officer, department, board, or bureau of the municipality affected by any decision of the administrative officer. Such appeal shall be taken within a reasonable time, as provided by the rules of the board, by filing with the officer from whom the appeal is taken and with the board of adjustment a notice of appeal specifying the grounds thereof. The officer from whom the appeal is taken shall forthwith transmit to the board all the papers constituting the record upon which the action appealed from was taken.

An appeal stays all proceedings in furtherance of the action appealed from, unless the officer from whom the appeal is taken certifies to the board of adjustment after the notice of appeal shall have been filed with him that by reason of facts stated in the certificate a stay would, in his opinion, cause imminent peril to life or property. In such case proceedings shall not be stayed otherwise than by a restraining order which may be granted by the board of adjustment or by a court of record on application on notice to the officer from whom the appeal is taken and on due cause shown.

The board of adjustment shall fix a reasonable time for the hearing of the appeal, give public notice thereof, as well as due notice to the parties in interest, and decide the same within a reasonable time. Upon the hearing any party may appear in person or by agent or by attorney.

The board of adjustment shall have the following powers:

1. To hear and decide appeals where it is alleged there is error in any order, requirement, decision, or determination made by an administrative official in the enforcement of this act or of any ordinance adopted pursuant thereto.

2. To hear and decide special exceptions to the terms of the ordinance upon which such board is required to pass under such ordinance.

3. To authorize upon appeal in specific cases such variance from the terms of the ordinance as will not be contrary to the public interest, where, owing to special conditions, a literal enforcement of the provisions of the ordinance will result in unnecessary hardship, and so that the spirit of the ordinance shall be observed and substantial justice done.

In exercising the above-mentioned powers such board may, in conformity with the provisions of this act, reverse or affirm, wholly or partly, or may modify the order, requirement, decision, or determination appealed from and may make such order, requirement, decision, or determination as ought to be made, and to that end shall have all the powers of the officer from whom the appeal is taken.

The concurring vote of four members of the board shall be necessary to reverse any order, requirement, decision, or determination of any such administrative official, or to decide in favor of the applicant on any matter upon which it is required to pass under any such ordinance, or to effect any variation in such ordinance.

Any person or persons, jointly or severally, aggrieved by any decision of the board of adjustment, or any taxpayer, or any officer, department, board, or bureau of the municipality, may present to a court of record a petition, duly verified, setting forth that such decision is illegal, in whole or in part, specifying the grounds of the illegality. Such petition shall be presented to the court within 30 days after the filing of the decision in the office of the board.

Upon the presentation of such petition the court may allow a writ of certiorari directed to the board of adjustment to review such decision of the board of adjustment and shall prescribe therein the time within which a return thereto must be made and served upon the relator's attorney, which shall not be less than 10 days and may be extended by the court. The allowance of the writ shall not stay proceedings upon the decision appealed from, but the court may, on application, on notice to the board and on due cause shown, grant a restraining order.

The board of adjustment shall not be required to return the original papers acted upon by it, but it shall be sufficient to return certified or sworn copies thereof or of such portions thereof as may be called for by such writ. The return shall concisely set forth such other facts as may be pertinent and material to show the grounds of the decision appealed from and shall be verified.

If, upon the hearing, it shall appear to the court that testimony is necessary for the proper disposition of the matter, it may take evidence or appoint a referee to take such evidence as it may direct and report the same to the court with his findings of fact and conclusions of law, which shall constitute a part of the proceedings upon which the determination of the court shall be made. The court may reverse or affirm, wholly or partly, or may modify the decision brought up for review.

Costs shall not be allowed against the board unless it shall appear to the court that it acted with gross negligence, or in bad faith, or with malice in making the decision appealed from.

All issues in any proceeding under this section shall have preference over all other civil actions and proceedings.

SECTION 8. ENFORCEMENT AND REMEDIES.—The local legislative body may provide by ordinance for the enforcement of this act and of any ordinance or regulation made thereunder. A violation of this act or of such ordinance or regulation is hereby declared to be a misdemeanor, and such local legislative body may provide for the punishment thereof by fine or imprisonment or both. It is also empowered to provide civil penalties for such violation.

In case any building or structure is erected, constructed, reconstructed, altered, repaired, converted, or maintained, or any building, structure, or land is used in violation of this act or of any ordinance or other regulation made under authority conferred hereby, the proper local authorities of the municipality, in addition to other remedies, may institute any appropriate action or proceedings to prevent such unlawful erection, construction, reconstruction, alteration, repair, conversion, maintenance, or use, to restrain, correct, or abate such violation, to prevent the occupancy of said building, structure, or land, or to prevent any illegal act, conduct, business, or use in or about such premises.

SECTION 9. CONFLICT WITH OTHER LAWS.—Wherever the regulations made under authority of this act require a greater width or size of yards, courts, or other open spaces, or require a lower height of building or less number of stories, or require a greater percentage of lot to be left unoccupied, or impose other higher standards than are required in any other statute or local ordinance or regulation, the provisions of the regulations made under authority of this act shall govern. Wherever the provisions of any other statute or local ordinance or regulation require a lower height of building or a lesser number of stories, or require a greater percentage of lot to be left unoccupied, or impose other higher standards than are required by the regulations made under authority of this act, the provisions of such statute or local ordinance or regulation shall govern.

APPENDIX B

A Note on Schedules of District Regulations

The three parts of a zoning ordinance—the text, the official map, and the schedule of district regulations—are inseparable. We have attempted the standardization of the text. While standardization of a schedule of district regulations is not essential (and would be most difficult to accomplish), the elements involved in drafting such a schedule can be suggested.

Form.—In form, the schedule of district regulations is best organized in columns. The following column heads laid out at the top of the large sheet and reading from left to right have been useful to us:

Districts and Intent (Include the district nomenclature and a short statement of the reason for creating the district.)

Uses and Structures (Four sub-columns here)
Permitted Principal Uses and Structures
Permitted Accessory Uses and Structures
Special Exceptions: After public notice and hearing and appropriate conditions and safegards, the Board of Adjustment may permit, as special exceptions:
Prohibited Uses and Structures

Minimum Lot Requirements—Area and Width

Minimum Yard Requirements—Depth of front and rear yard, width of side yard

Maximum Lot Coverage by all Buildings

Maximum Height of Structures

Minimum Off-Street Parking and Off-Street Loading Requirements

Limitations on Signs—No signs intended to be read from off the premises shall be permitted except:

Notes (This column provides space for explanatory and other material which would be too lengthy for inclusion in the main body of the schedule.)

If the schedule of district regulations is not to be set in type and printed, it may be typewritten on strips of drafting paper, taped together with clear book-mending tape, and run through an Ozalid machine. This practice, in small towns where great numbers need not be printed, greatly reduces costs.

Comments on the Columns. Districts and Intent. A statement of the intended purpose of each zoning classification is necessary—and extremely difficult to write. Obviously, such statements aid the courts in interpretation in event of litigation. Of greater importance, the statements of intent help in the drafting of the ordinance, particularly in determining whether specific uses *really* belong in a particular classification. It is much easier to decide, for example, what business uses are to be allowed in a specific commercial district if there is a clear statement of intent for that particular district. Drafters should not hesitate to spend a great amount of time on these statements of intent.

Permitted Principal Uses and Structures. Uses listed in this column are permitted *as of right*. This means that an applicant for a building permit *must* be given a permit if he meets the other requirements of the ordinance, *e.g.*, yards, setbacks, and so forth.

Permitted Accessory Uses and Structures. Normally, the statements in this column are general. Occasionally some specific statement may be desired. Some cities, for example, may wish to consider a private swimming pool as an accessory use to a residence and should so indicate.

Special Exceptions. We have already discussed the utility of the special exception and its administration. In this column would be listed those uses for a particular district that are to be permissible as special exceptions after notice and hearing before the board of adjustment. A city might wish, for example, to permit hospitals as special exceptions in single-family residential zones rather than permitting them as of right in such zones.

Prohibited Uses and Structures. Again, statements in this column are normally general. Some specific prohibitions will usually be necessary. Where it is desired for example, to prohibit residences in industrial zones or certain commercial zones, a statement to that effect would appear in this column. For residential districts, the statement would usually be one prohibiting all uses not permitted or permissible as special exceptions.

Minimum Lot Requirements—Area and Width. In this column are recorded the minimum lot requirements. Residential uses and certain institutional uses will certainly require setting out such requirements. Sometimes such requirements are set for certain commercial uses such as filling stations. On the other hand, minimum lot requirements are usually not set out for industrial uses and, quite frequently, are not set out for general commercial uses.

Minimum Yard Requirements. The requirements for depth of front and rear yards and the width of side yards would be set out here. Yard requirements are a "must" for residential and institutional uses. Front yard requirements are usually imperative in most commercial and industrial zones. Side yard requirements are less common for industrial and commercial uses and often are not necessary at all.

Maximum Lot Coverage by All Buildings. Maximum lot coverage requirements are one way of ensuring adequate light and air. The actual percentages will vary greatly from city to city. For multiple-family structures, the rule generally is "the taller the building the smaller the maximum percentage of lot coverage at ground level."

Maximum Height of Structures. This column is self-explanatory. Different heights may be set for structures housing different uses.

Minimum Off-Street Parking and Off-Street Loading Requirements. Emphasis on the automobile is constantly forcing such minimum requirements upward. We have recently been involved in the writing of ordinances where one and a half or two off-street parking spaces were required for *each* dwelling unit in an apartment house; not too many years ago one space was considered sufficient. In this day and age, no residential, commercial, institutional, or industrial building should be erected without adequate provision for off-street parking and, where necessary, off-street loading. Drafters should carefully categorize the various types of commercial and industrial uses; some require less space than others. A single standard for *all* commercial activity would undoubtedly be invalid.

Limitations on Signs. Types and sizes of signs for each district must be in accordance with the uses of the district. If churches are permitted in single-family residential districts, for example, then provisions must be made for bulletin type signs of a maximum allowable size for such churches. Formulas will have to be established for calculating the maximum allowable size and number of on-site advertising signs in commercial districts and restrictions set out on type and location. Other formulas will be necessary for size and number of off-site advertising signs.

Notes. In this column is placed any explanatory material that cannot, for any reason, be included in the main body of the schedule. In many instances, this column will not be needed.

The Substance of the Schedule of District Regulations. It is the actual regulations for the various zoning classifications that most distinguish—or ought to distinguish—one community from another. As a zoning ordinance is drafted, its authors will want to bear in mind constantly that they are drafting the ordinance to implement a comprehensive plan—or they ought to be! The zoning classifications that they establish in the schedule of district regulations and the requirements that they set out for the various districts should each have a reason for being, and the reason should be one that can be defended.

There is often a tendency, particularly among those not too familiar with planning and the drafting of zoning ordinances, to create too many classifications with but minute variations between the classifications. A more judicious grouping of uses, with critical questions being asked as to whether or not uses are or are not incompatible, careful utilization of the special exception technique, and a recognition that diversity in use is not, *per se,* undesirable, will usually result in an ordinance with fewer, but more meaningful, classifications.

Most cities will require at least three types of zoning districts based on land use: (1) residential districts, (2) commercial districts, and (3) industrial districts. Smaller and specialized cities may not require industrial districts. There are at least three cases, to our knowledge, where zoning for residential purposes *only* has been held valid by the courts.

Nevertheless, these three general classifications will provide a starting point in most cases. Drafters will want to decide whether more than one category of single-family residential districts is required. A caution is again offered against "over categorization." Traditionally, most ordinances have contained a "duplex" or "two-family" category. We have not been recommending such a separate category to the cities which we serve as consultants. Any casual study of the average "duplex" district will show that 90 or 95 per cent of the dwelling units in such a classification are single-family. As an alternative, we have been recommending one or two "general residential" classifications within which two-family and multi-family units can be erected.

In addition to residential use in residential categories, decisions must be made as to other uses that will be permitted, such as churches, schools, parks, and so forth. Some drafters may decide to use the special exception category for home occupations, rather than permitting them as of right.

Most small- or medium-sized cities will require at least two commercial classifications, and sometimes more. The basic distinction is between the automotive oriented commercial uses and those uses which are not (at least not to so great a degree) automotive oriented.

Industrial zones should utilize the newer techniques of control by what are known as "performance standards." Older ordinances attempted to regulate land use for industrial purposes by specifying the types of products that might be manufactured in the various zones. With newer methods for control and measurement of noise, smoke, odors, electrical interference, heat, humidity, and other deleterious effects of industrial activity, there is little reason to regulate industrial location on the basis of the product to be manufactured. The important thing is to control the exterior effects of the activity.

In addition to the traditional classifications based on residential, commercial, and industrial use, specialized districts may be required. Agricultural districts are now more common than they once were. Flood plain districts which exclude uses that would be harmed by periodic flooding are being written into ordinances in those areas requiring such protection; residential uses, for example, are not allowed in such districts.

In drafting a schedule of district regulations, it is wise to remember that commercial and industrial activity needs protection against residential intrusion as much as residential uses deserve protection against commercial and industrial activity.

In the older concept of zoning, the most restrictive classification was the single-family residential one. As one proceeded down the line of the ordinances, all uses were cumulative for the districts; the lowest zone (usually the "heavy" industrial zone) allowed every use found in all the other zones.

This concept has now been thoroughly discredited, though unfortunately not yet completely abandoned. Residential and institutional uses can validly be excluded from industrial zones under court decisions now controlling in most states. This concept is known as "exclusive zoning," though the term is a bit misleading. We might note, parenthetically, that exclusion of residential uses from at least some of the commercial classifications tends to cut down requests for rezoning of residential land to commercial, since one of the speculative elements has thereby been removed. If an owner knows that he cannot fall back on a residential sale if his land is rezoned commercial he tends to think a bit before requesting speculative commercial zoning.

Persons seeking further aid on this topic as well as information on the drawing of district boundaries are referred to AMERICAN SOCIETY OF PLANNING OFFICIALS, PLANNING ADVISORY SERVICE INFORMATION REPORT No. 136, July 1960.

APPENDIX C

A Note on Indexing Zoning Ordinances

Every zoning ordinance should be indexed. The cost, in time and in printing, is negligible. The profits, in time saved for those who must administer the ordinance and for the public generally, more than justify the cost.

It is strange that so many ordinances are not indexed. Some do not even have a table of contents. Administrators and citizens are left to their own devices in trying to find the portion of the ordinance that concerns them at the moment.

Every ordinance should have a table of contents. This table should indicate the section headings of the text, much in the manner that the Table of Contents of the model text does.

An index at the back of an ordinance can be prepared after the ordinance has been finally typed or printed. Such an index is not a legal part of the ordinance, nor should it be. It constitutes an informal guide to finding one's way in material which, to the average citizen, is more than apt to be confusing.

One further indexing device should be noted. Cross references are a great aid. Again, the time and effort needed to prepare them is negligible. Cross references should be references to other sections or subsections, not page numbers. They can thus be prepared as a part of the final copy and set in type or typewritten as a part of the end product. Cross references, where necessary, should appear at the end of the appropriate section or subsection. They should be enclosed in brackets or parentheses to set them off from the text itself. If the ordinance is set in type, they should be set in a smaller size type.

All persons who must have recourse to a zoning ordinance will rise up and call him blessed who prepares for the ordinances indices of the type noted.